No One Could Know wi
choices the author made
you to reflect on the thing ....
own life. The courage Kristan shows in sharing her heart in this
autobiography is truly admirable. As a longtime friend dating
back to our childhood, she truly encapsulated the secret, for as
close as we were, even I did not know.

—Kim Carpenter, Author of the #1 New York Times Bestselling
Book, *The Vow*

My chest tightened and my heart hurt as Kristan shared her life
experiences—the choices, the consequences, and the salvation.
No One Could Know is a book that I will share with my daughter.
It is a beautiful work of literature that will facilitate many
discussions and, I hope, inspire others to carefully consider
their life choices.

—Iowa State Senator Joni Ernst

No One Could Know is the true, heart-breaking story of love,
pregnancy, abortion, guilt, religious cover up and the power of
God's truth, mercy, forgiveness, and freedom. This is a must
read for every student, mom, dad, and Christian leader, as well
as those who have experienced the guilt and shame of a past
abortion.

—Beth Jones, Author and Cofounder of Valley Family Church,
Kalamazoo, Michigan

No One Could Know

Kristan Gray

WestBow
PRESS
A DIVISION OF THOMAS NELSON

WestBow Press books may be ordered through booksellers or by contacting:

WestBow Press
A Division of Thomas Nelson
1663 Liberty Drive
Bloomington, IN 47403
www.westbowpress.com
1 (866) 928-1240

Because of the dynamic nature of the Internet, any web addresses or
links contained in this book may have changed since publication and
may no longer be valid. The views expressed in this work are solely those
of the author and do not necessarily reflect the views of the publisher,
and the publisher hereby disclaims any responsibility for them.

Any people depicted in stock imagery provided by Thinkstock are
models, and such images are being used for illustrative purposes only.
Certain stock imagery © Thinkstock.

ISBN: 978-1-4908-2025-5 (sc)
ISBN: 978-1-4908-2024-8 (hc)
ISBN: 978-1-4908-2026-2 (e)

Library of Congress Control Number: 2013922950

Printed in the United States of America.

WestBow Press rev. date: 12/26/2013

Dedication

To all of you who have found yourselves in an "unwanted" pregnancy situation, yet have chosen to let your baby live.

To those who, like me, chose "the easy way" out and are living with regret.

This book is also dedicated to the One who saved me, Jesus Christ; our God, who revealed himself to me as "Father"; and the Holy Spirit, my Comforter.

My story now belongs to Him.

Contents

Acknowledgements

A humble thank-you to those of you who support me with your friendship and love: My four wonderful parents, Phyllis and Larry Owen, and Joe and Lainna Hill; my project advisor whom I met when we were in first grade, Kim Carpenter, and his wife, Krickitt. He's the man whose story of dedication to his wife became a best-selling book and movie, *The Vow*. To the Kenneth E. Hagin and Buddy and Pat Harrison families, and all of my Rhema Bible Training College instructors who spoon-fed me the Word of God and whose transparent lives have been a living testimony.

My deepest gratitude to the God-given women in my life who sharpen my soul: Ginny Houser, Haley Schurz, Chris Peterson, Carolyn Clark, Cindy Hoskins, Beth Jones, and Rhonda Rogers; and to LeAnn Hawthorne who was the first to financially support this project. I covet your prayers, and you have mine. The next coffee is on me.

To my husband, Scott, and my kids—Ryan, Matt, and Haley. As Buddy Harrison used to say, "If you make a mess in your britches and fall down in it, I'll still love you, stink and all."

Introduction

I had an abortion.

It's that plain. It's in no way simple to say, but there it is.

I was also raped.

In that order: abortion—then rape.

Actually, I got pregnant the first time I ever had sex. I was sixteen. Six weeks later when I got the abortion, it was also my seventeenth birthday.

About a year later came the rape—from a "friend."

I now have three children of my own and have *no greater joy* than being their mother. Motherhood is the most important job on the planet—I am convinced. I am so deeply grateful that I could physically bear children after the abortion—not everyone can. To those of you who cannot, I can't begin to express my deepest sympathies to you. I'm so sorry. I so passionately wish I could turn back the clock. I wish I could reach every single one of you in the world who has experienced an abortion—whether you are on my side of the story or on "Brock's." I pray that you find the healing in your souls that I am eternally grateful to have in mine. It is available.

CHAPTER 1

Sweet Sixteen and Never Been Kissed

"I f you're 'sweet sixteen and never been kissed,' I'll buy you a gold watch for your sixteenth birthday!" As a little girl, that frequent promise from my fabulous mom created a fairy-tale-princess impression in my mind. I imagined how wonderful life would be when I blew out that sixteenth candle on my traditional German chocolate birthday cake!

Being sixteen became a fanciful dream every time I played with my Barbie doll three-story townhouse with the drawstring elevator. You may remember similar years of wonder from your own childhood—days spent dreaming as you played things like my resourceful third grade classmate Laura and I did.

Barbie's home in my bedroom closet was decorated with furniture carefully crafted out of scraps from Mom's sewing remnants and recycled toilet paper tubes—to accompany the pink inflatable couch and chair. Every time brunette Barbie cruised my green shag carpet in her pink convertible, I daydreamed about flipping my own long brown hair and dangling a gold watch from my wrist. Barbie was always celebrating her pretend sixteenth birthday with Sun-Lovin' Malibu Barbie and her boyfriend Ken at the swimming pool.

The only qualifications any of Barbie's suitors needed were to be able to rescue her from being trapped on the third-floor roof by plastic Godzilla, and provide her with better furniture than she could come up with during a DIY weekend with Laura's Barbies. And, when that first kiss came—it had to be magical. After all, Barbie was sixteen and old enough to kiss.

Life with Laura as my friend was always full of adventure. We thought of ourselves as well beyond our age of eight. One particular hot summer day in our southwest Utah desert town, we decided we'd try to be as cool as our cowboy parents and take up smoking.

We knew right where to find cigarettes. There were always plenty of them left in ash trays around Laura's dad's office at the ranch. The trouble was that the butts we found had been puffed all the way to the filter before being snubbed out.

We had to dig deeper if we were going to find our own "coffin nails," so we went on a serious "ciggie" hunt that lasted for hours. We looked in trashcans, pickup trucks, drawers, closets, and cabinets—and beneath couch cushions—but turned up only some loose change and a pack of matches.

My crafty colleague was not to be denied, however. With me in her shadow, she pranced off to the office bathroom and yanked two paper towel squares from the holder on the wall above the black metal trash can. Then, with me in her shadow, she tromped off to the horse corrals. Laura pulled a piece of bark off one of the fence posts that formed part of a gray mare's stall. With my hand shaking, I copied her motion, and in one fell swoop, I had myself a two-by-four-inch stogie to wrap in the paper towel she held out toward me.

Laura lit hers first, then promptly lit mine, and for a split second—before the blaze reached Las Vegas hotel rooftop heights—I felt powerfully grown up. I planted one hand on my waist and with the other hand, I held out the "cigarette" in fine Phyllis Diller flamboyant Hollywood style, pretending that I was holding a twelve-inch cigarette holder like Phyllis's.

I took one puff of the "stogie" and black smoke filled my lungs as the fire grew hotter and closer to my fingers. I choked several times and threw the flaming Bounty and all its "quicker picker upper" power into the six-inch-deep sand at my feet. Then, with one stomp of the Justin cowgirl boots I was wearing with my pink and yellow plaid shorts, I put that fire out. "Real" cowboys like the Marlboro Man smoked, and I knew that if I ever got to kiss someone, it wouldn't be a smoker. So, right there in that stable, I gave up cigarettes—and cowboys.

Still, for one fire-breathing moment, I'd felt sixteen, that enchanted age when girls were finally "grown up" enough to wear real homecoming dance dresses and not merely play "dress-up" in their mom's 1963 pastel yellow chiffon dress. Sixteen, when every dance was attended with Prince Charming and life was just as fulfilling as every little girl dreamed it should be. I could hear my mom's voice trailing off in the sunset in my head, "… sweet sixteen … never been kissed … gold watch…."

As it turned out, my first kiss was planted on my lips in the gymnasium at Woodward Elementary School's gymnasium in St. George, Utah, when I was twelve. The Gideon's International organization visited Mr. Hudson's sixth grade classroom that day and handed out little red Bibles. Some friends came up with a brilliant idea to sneak off after lunch and use the Bibles in a wedding ceremony. What else were we to do with them? So, with Luke Parks officiating the double wedding, Kate Harris and Ron Goldstein, and Cody Smith and I said, "I do" and kissed a supremely awkward kiss.

It was nothing like I had imagined. I didn't hear Karen Carpenter's voice singing, "Why do birds suddenly appear, every time you are near?"[1] or see fireworks like Bobby Brady did when he kissed Millicent on *The Brady Bunch*.

My heart pounded against my ribs and my shaking palms pooled with sweat, thanks to the peer pressure other sixth graders were dishing out that year. It seemed like lunch break and recess were daily wracked with expectation to meet behind a building to kiss. I wondered, *"Is this what being a girlfriend is supposed to be like?* I would have rather been playing dodgeball. *Is this how boyfriends are supposed to act? In elementary school? Why did we have to kiss?*

Because I was twelve instead of sixteen when I was kissed for the first time, I'd sacrificed a gold watch for the deal—and it wasn't even that great. It was clumsy and pressure ridden. And once I had crossed that line, it felt like there was no going back. It seemed like kissing was expected from then on. After all, that's what boyfriends and girlfriends did. Didn't they? Didn't *everyone?*

Weren't real relationships supposed to be unpretentious and straight forward? I started to miss being in third grade when things were clear—like the note Cody had passed to me during Mr. Graham's third grade reading class. On a piece of red construction paper with torn edges, he'd written the sweetest thing I'd ever seen. "I like you. Do you like me? Circle *yes* or *no*."

I wasn't so sure about the new expectations. What was with all this kissing clutter clouding simplistic relationships? I was better at passing straight-forward notes and just hanging out playing kickball. Those rules were clear.

Soon after we got "married," we all found different relationships. Perhaps Cody could tell in my kisses that I'd rather be slugging a softball bat or solving math equations than kissing.

Another shady encounter I had with sixth grade peer pressure was when "all the other kids" were crossing the street to sneak to the candy store during recess. I didn't want to cross the street. We weren't supposed to leave the school yard, and other than my third grade stint of rolling my own cigarette, I was an upstanding citizen. But that street seemed all too easy. If only we didn't have that barrier command, *don't*. There were no crosswalk guards to distract, no fences to climb, no alarms to disable, and no laser beams to limbo beneath that would otherwise keep us inside our little boundary.

Miss "Candice E. Ahmbizzy," the librarian, served as the perfect playground monitor from whom to escape, because she was always distracted. She relished sweetly pointing out nature to the small group of second graders still interested in that sort of thing.

When two of my pals had had enough of the mundane break-time customs, they were certain Judd's was the place to be—and they knew I had fifteen cents in my pocket left over from lunch. That was just enough money to buy each of us a five cent sour sucker.

The more they talked, the more those suckers with orange on top and yellow on the bottom danced around my head like Sugar Plum Fairies—taunting, luring me to jump that asphalt and take one little taste of sour on a hot day. The gauntlet lay right there in the middle of West Tabernacle Street, and I picked it up. I followed the girls around the big oak tree and we ran hard and fast, right into that candy store with the breeze blowing in behind us.

The sugar-coated sugar on top of the plastic stick didn't last long, so the evidence was promptly disposed in time to hear the first bell calling us to the right side of the tracks.

We never got caught sneaking across the street, and we were never caught kissing behind buildings or in the gymnasium. That's the thing about peer pressure, sometimes you and Miss or Mr. Vice Grip are the only ones to know what was done, and a secret is lugged around in the sugar-coated corners of your mind the rest of your life.[2] And, the adults in your world don't always know what's going on behind closed doors.

Kind of like my having an abortion...no one could know...

CHAPTER 2

The Morning Side of the Mountain

J unior high whizzed by without my having a boyfriend, per se. Oh, there were crushes all right but none that ever materialized into a romantic relationship. I was frizzy-haired from bad perms and my teeth looked as if someone had rolled a handful of molars into my mouth like they were Las-Vegas dice, letting my choppers land where ever they would. In my mind, my Rocky Mountain jeans and jelly shoes just didn't seem as cool on me as they did on the other girls. Braces came in the middle of the seventh grade as did gallons of Love's Baby Soft perfume and a whole lot of Maybelline mascara from the pink tube with the green lid. Nothing, however, really covered my freckle-faced fear of getting too close to a boy.

"Fearless" Frank Barretto was the Friday-night radio disc jockey at our groovy radio station, KJYN. (Frank lived for skydiving on weekends, hence the name.) Since I knew "Fearless" as the dad of my next-door-neighbor-friend Shelby, I felt very comfortable calling the station's hotline and making song requests. Usually my appeal was for him to play "Morning Side of the Mountain" by Donny and Marie Osmond. It's a deeply lonely and emotionally torturous song that would leave me in tears, aching to find that special someone whose kiss would—as Donny and Marie sang in another song—"make the world go away."[3] That was a kiss I would take.

It wasn't that the world as I knew it was anything I wanted to escape—I had a great family. Sure my parents had split several years earlier, but in turn, I acquired two outstanding stepparents who each made life great for my respective parents. I'm fortunate to have four parents who love me and siblings with whom I love to spend time. A full brother, stepbrother, a half-brother, and a half-sister complete our family. Throw a host of kids and grandkids into the mix now, and every family reunion becomes YouTube-comedy worthy. I'm one of the blessed ones that way, but when I was in junior high, I longed to have a love of my own and a kiss that meant something more than what it had felt like in that elementary school gym. I wanted a Friday-night skating partner who could spin circles with me in the middle of the rink under the mirrored disco ball. I knew he had to be out there somewhere—I didn't think he was in my small school.

In "Morning Side of the Mountain," Donny sings, "There was a girl, there was a boy. If they had met they might have found a world of joy, but he lived on the morning side of the mountain and she lived on the twilight side of the hill …"

Then Marie laments that the two never met and never kissed, so … "they will never know what happiness they've missed …[4]

I knew there had to be someone out there who didn't mind a freckled face, and who loved exploring my beloved Rocky Mountains. I yearned to be on a great guy's team who wanted to be with me just because he liked me, not just because he wanted to kiss me. As much as I loved Donny and Marie's song, their words—"For all we know our love is just a kiss away"—did not make enough sense to me. Shouldn't you love the fella *before* you kiss him? I knew there had to be someone out there, but he was likely on the morning side of the mountain, so I wanted to move there.

Soon I was the new girl in high school—I moved with my family back to our home state of New Mexico, only three days before my sophomore year of high school began. The braces came off, and I became quite handy with hot rollers to tame my frizzy perms. I also became a skilled mall shopper.

We were only a few weeks into school when one of the baseball players invited me to some of the homecoming-week activities.

My first date ever was mangled by my first *most embarrassing moment* ever. Mark Adamson was shy and sweet and seemed as nervous as I was—but not just about being with me. He'd borrowed his sister's little red Datsun B-210 hatchback and had saved all his pennies until his dollars added up to buy enough gas to get me to the Sonic Drive-In for a burger.

Obsessing over which Dillard's outfit to wear on our first date, I settled on a loosely knit, thick cream sweater over a red polo shirt, with the collar sticking up, coupled with Jordache blue jeans and brown leather knee-high boots.

Mark obsessed about keeping his sister's car clean. He insisted that we sit on towels lest we drop our greasy fast food on her car seats.

I ordered a bacon cheeseburger and a cherry limeade. I wasn't shy about eating in front of a guy. My jazz, tap, and ballet dance classes twice a week and cycling all over town kept my hunger at optimum teenage levels. I was hungry enough to eat a hot fudge sundae after the burger, but didn't want to break my penny-pinching date on our first night out.

Waiting for our food to arrive, my stomach roared like a Grizzly. I nervously laughed it off, grateful for the diversion of the roller-skating waitress at the window with our dinner.

My drink was the perfect blend of carbonation and sugary syrup for my cotton mouth and cooled my nerves. It took me a second, but I realized exactly why I cooled so quickly—my Styrofoam cup was leaking cherry syrup all over my leg and Mark's sister's car! I had poked the straw plumb through the bottom of the cup! My date blew a gasket, fearing what his sister would do about the red drink spilled on her carpet. I was mortified and felt horrible for being the one to ruin his chance of ever borrowing her car again.

I imagined the high-school rumor mill abuzz with what a bad date I had been and feared I'd never know a second date— with anyone. I'd surely grow to be the old spinster who lived in the creepy house on the highest hill in town. You know, the house overgrown with unkempt landscaping and whose tenant had only experienced a pretend marriage way back in the sixth grade.

I threw open the car door, shook out the few remaining drops onto the ground, and burst inside Sonic's doors as I hollered, *"Help! I need napkins, please!"*

I didn't see the man standing behind the glass door. The unsuspecting guy was washing the floor with a hose, and I blindsided him with the door! I was glad he wasn't bruised or bleeding and that the glass was intact. I couldn't cause any more damage!

After my apologies, the fry cook peeled himself away from the grill and pointed to a pile of napkins to my right. But I had to watch my step—I was *not* going to fall; *that* would be embarrassing. But the entire four-foot stack of napkins landed right in the standing puddle of dirty water on the floor!

Could a date go any more wrongly? I didn't want to go back to the car. I was humiliated and wished my mom could pick me up and take me home. I did my best to clean up the mess I'd made. It must not have been too bad in Mark's eyes, because—much to my surprise—he asked me out for a second date. At least I wasn't being judged on my Styrofoam-cup-handling skills, freckles didn't scare him away—and he hadn't even tried to kiss me. Everything was cool. He liked me—for *me.*

Mark and I spent several of the following evenings with other classmates during the week's special activities. I was looking forward to the homecoming dance and getting to wear the white Gunne Sax dress I'd found while shopping with Mom. I thought it looked much better on me than her tattered pastel yellow dress that I'd worn out and repaired many times during my days spent playing "dress up," dreaming of this very occasion.

"When I pick you up for the dance Saturday night, I have a surprise for you," Mark said. "Be ready at sunset."

I'd been ready for hours. My body was drenched in Heaven's Scent perfume this time, my breath was ablaze with cinnamon Close-Up toothpaste, and my feathered hair was so firmly coated with Stiff Stuff hairspray it was like a new nonstick skillet. I sat in the white plush swivel chair by the front door and watched the road for his car.

Mark pulled into our country gravel driveway right on time. (In his sister's car again—this time I'd be more careful!) He stepped out of the vehicle and I bolted to hide behind the door. It seemed like it took him forever to ring the doorbell.

There it was … I waited a few seconds as if I were coming from the back of the house instead of peeping through the sheer curtains.

"I stepped in something in the grass," he said as I opened the door.

Great. He'd found the one area of the yard our dog did her business. I was glad to know that the smell that had wafted to my nose didn't originate with him. So much for my "scent of heaven" aromatherapy.

Leaving him outside, I dashed to the kitchen and found my mom.

"You're not going to believe this…" I began, and asked her what to do.

We got Mark's shoe cleaned off and he lured me to the edge of the porch. He handed my mom a white tea-towel to blindfold me and made her promise she wouldn't let me peek from underneath it. I waited impatiently, trying to imagine what on earth he could be doing.

Whooosh….I heard what sounded like a hot-air balloon rising to a new altitude, and desperately wanted to cheat the tea towel to see what was happening in my yard a few steps down.

Mom threatened, *"Don't* look!"

Next I heard what sounded like sparks and began to wonder if our grass was on fire when Mark bounded up the steps and pulled the covering from my eyes.

It was beautiful … the most romantic thing I had ever seen. The sunset that evening was a stunning backdrop of purples and oranges and reds to the green oak-tree leaves that hinted of autumn's more splendorous colors to come. There in the grass stood a crystal vase of long-stemmed red roses sprinkled with tiny white baby's breath and brilliant green leaves. Surrounding the vase was a wreath of Fourth of July sparklers stuck into the ground, all going off at the same time. Mark had lit them with a welder's torch, so they could all begin fairly close to the same time and fade to the end of their spectacular presentation in unison.

Mark, Mom, and I stood speechless, wrapped up in the cool September breeze and basked in the beauty of the moment. I was impressed that he wasn't only romantic, but boldly so in front of my mom.

As we stood there, something else caught my eye—our two quarter horses, a dappled gray and a chestnut, had been at the fence taking in the event as well. But it was the motion of Nan, our nanny goat, rounding the corner of the house that drew my eyes from my delightful gift. Apparently my goat was in awe of the roses too and was determined to get her fair share. Without stopping for permission, she bee-lined straight for the roses and began to eat them!

We ran to pull her away, but Mark stopped with a jolt and asked, "What is *that?*"

Oh, my word. Seriously? How many embarrassing moments would I have as a teenager? I really wanted to know the answer to that question, so I could see an end to them. As if my long-stemmed-rose-eating, romance-crushing goat wasn't bad enough! This was the worst.

While this fiasco was a byproduct of country living, the lifestyle also has tremendous advantages. For instance, every morning I'd wake up with a smile as I'd hear our horses whinnying outside my bedroom window. My greatest marvel was at the Canadian Geese that flew in formation over our house near the river, giving me their morning honk of hellos. I loved it—everything about it. I loved living just far enough outside the city to have privacy, open spaces, and a place to keep large rodeo-style pets, yet be close enough to dash to the mall at a moment's notice. But as country folks know, living so close to timber and open fields has disadvantages too—like coyotes, for example.

Coyotes had recently ambushed several neighboring animals, and unfortunately, Nan the nanny goat had been the victim of a recent attack. The best things my parents could find on hand to doctor her shredded back leg were athletic tape and a feminine maxi-pad for a bandage! There it was in plain sight on the back end of my goat for my boyfriend to see. As much as my heart was moved by Mark's romance, my feet were now moved with humiliation. I grabbed my purse and my date and we raced to the dance, leaving Mom to take care of the goat and my partially eaten flowers.

My relationship with Mark didn't last much past homecoming. He was nice and thoughtful—and forgiving! I guess "it" just wasn't there, but he left me with the dream that there are real guys out there just as dreamy as some in the movies but who script their own romances. Mark simply wasn't the one I clicked with for a long-term relationship. For all I knew, the guy I longed to have a relationship with still lived on the "morning side of the mountain" and I was still on the "twilight side of the hill."

CHAPTER 3

My Sweet-Sixteenth Birthday

I don't even remember my sixteenth birthday.

For the life of me, all I know about that invisible line across the great divide is that I must have had a birthday cake with homemade German Chocolate frosting and vanilla ice cream. I always do.

It's such a shame I don't remember a thing about *turning* sixteen. I always looked forward to birthdays, because they were such a big production in my family. I've always treasured having triumphant get-togethers with aunts, uncles, cousins, and grandparents for each person's celebration. But, I don't like that my big day happens to be only three weeks after Christmas, because it's always a dreadfully long time before the next gift-getting extravaganza rolls around.

I do know that on my sixteenth, I received the long anticipated gold watch, even though Mom knew I *had* been kissed before I blew out that sixteenth candle—not by Mark, but later, by a different boyfriend.

Cameron was an extraordinary kisser.

We met simply in passing—in a horde of teenagers clamoring for space in the congested hallway of the school's science building. He sauntered in my direction—his gorgeous black-brown eyes locked onto mine like heat-seeking missiles that then sucked me into them as he came closer. He kept staring right into my eyes, dismissing the hallway havoc around him. I'd never seen him before; I would have remembered a face—and a swagger—like that!

"Who-whooo-whoooooooo is *this* guy?" I wondered to myself. How had I never run into him before? I had *really* been missing out! He had to be a super hero—his power to make people melt could not be human.

"Hi, I'm Cameron Martino."

It spoke. That beautiful creature even spoke the same language I did, and he was speaking to *me!* Closely … he was standing very closely.

My face hurt and I realized the corners of mouth had been frozen in a smiling position since my eyes connected with his. I casually lifted my hand to release the lockjaw, and blushed.

I wish everyone could experience feeling that attractive to someone they find breath-taking. Our instant-Jell-O-pudding relationship was one everyone should experience at some point in their lives. It was an award-winning recipe: take a one-ton boy and a one-pint girl, put them in a hallway, add some froth between classes, and it's complete—and that simple.

Except for the parts where he was a Kiss-O-Maniac and every date was a Kiss-O-Rama.

Our first date was that very night. Something amazing happened that I thought only happened in fairy tales. Remember when Cinderella's mice turned into horses and her pumpkin turned into a golden carriage to take her to the ball? When the clock struck midnight, Cameron turned into an octopus. His hands were everywhere, and he whispered into my sensitive ear, "I want to make love to you."

I shoved him away, "I'm not like that!"

And then he said it.

"But, I love you!"

How did he "love" me when he hardly even knew me? Loved me how? He loved my freckles? My eyes that were only half the depth of brown as his? The way my hair feathered like Farrah Fawcett's? My dazzling wit? My brace-less teeth? My brilliant IQ? My goals for life and passion for the mountains? What could he possibly know about me well enough to "love"?

I was blown away at what was happening so fast—he kept kissing and kissing and kissing—and I liked it. He was incredibly suave and oh, so very, very handsome. And the best part of his being so model-esque? *I* was the one he wanted. *Me!*

Or was it necessarily *me* he wanted? We had only known each other less than twelve hours! I kissed back, but I abruptly stopped his roaming hands. It felt incredible to be tangled up in the arms of someone so strong. When they passed out muscles in the weight room, he got *all* the leftovers and surely stole lats, pecs, and biceps from the other guys in line. He was pushy that way. And I liked it. I was scared, but being in his arms felt amazing … as long as they stayed in the safe zone.

I could see why so many in our school were having sex. If what I was experiencing in the simple kiss-whisper-and-actively-cuddle phase, then sex had to be indescribably magnificent. I was nowhere close to being ready for anything like that, though—especially when it seemed like that was the only reason he wanted to be with me. Did he want to get to know my personality at all? I didn't even know this guy and he was telling me he loved me. What was his plan? Had he just eyed me at school as a "thing" to "do"? I was not a "thing," and I was not about to let him—or anyone—"do" anything to me.

Cameron and I dated a short while, with many kiss-fests, but thankfully he respected that kissing was as far as I was going to go. He sure acted like he loved me—for "me." We had a lot of fun together, but I broke up with him. It was all moving way too fast for me.

So there I was, "sweet sixteen" and I had been kissed—a lot.

The undeserved golden watch trophy was mine anyway.

I knew Mom felt that sixteen was some sort of passage into another dimension of humanness and something significant must be done to celebrate—she was good at celebrations. I just don't remember my sixteenth as being the colossal event that I'd expected in my childhood. Perhaps it was because I'd not really earned the fourteen carats that had been dangled in front of me all those years. I wasn't "gold watch worthy."

As a young girl I expected turning sixteen to be a grand affair in such a Scarlett-O'Hara-ball sort of way that I'd even dreamed of making a dress out of green velvet curtains like Scarlett had. But to this day, all I know is that I did get that coveted watch at some point. Perhaps that was the occasion I received the *Seventeen* magazine subscription.

The teen publications all promoted a physical relationship with "the boyfriend" and talked about sex. Most of their articles related to having some sort of romantic relationship with a guy, like, "What Movie Couple Are You and Your Boyfriend?" and "How to Turn His Head" or even "5 Different Ways to Kiss." They stimulated grandiose ideas of dating Harlequin-romance-novel style. The air-brushed shots of pretty girls in perfectly staged exotic lagoon locations that were splashed onto page after glossy page only served as measuring sticks of where I "should be" on the American adolescent scale.

I enjoyed picking up monthly makeup and wardrobe tips from the magazine, so I especially loved shopping trips with Mom—she is always fun to run around with. Every Saturday morning she'd wake me up with a cheery, "Get up, up, up, up, up—pancakes are ready! It's a bright new sun-shiny day! Clean your room and we'll go to Dillard's!"

But why couldn't my eyebrows be like Brooke Shields's caterpillary things or my hair as thick and wavy? Why couldn't my legs be tiny and tan instead of meaty and sunburned every summer? Would life really be more fun if I were blonde like so many of my Sun-In-using friends? After all, isn't looking like a super model the way to catch the best boyfriends? I was caught in a mind-altering web of comparing myself to others.

Why does society place expectations on teenagers that they "should" be dating someone anyway? Are they any less of a teen if they're flying solo? So many little boys are even teased with the probing question, "Do you have a girlfriend?" I always feel badly for children who are put on the spot with that question. A lingering expectation is surely imprinted in their psyche that they'll only be fully accepted by the world when they have a "little filly" on their arms.

Thankfully, my wise mother taught me that being beautiful on the inside is far more important than how I look on the outside. It didn't matter whether I dressed like a fashion plate in all the right makeup and accessories, or if I dressed in thick gray Russell sweats and black Converse high-top tennis shoes, or "waffle stomper" boots and button-up Levi jeans. The most important way to be beautiful was to know who I was internally and to shine from the inside out.

The trouble was, I had no idea who I was or who I even wanted to become. Mom always encouraged me that I could be whoever I wanted to be.

One day while standing in the kitchen, she asked me, "Would you rather be a jack-of-all-trades and master of none or a specialist in one thing?" That was something I had never thought about before.

"Kristan," she instructed, "you can go anywhere or do anything in the world that you set your mind to do."

I believed her.

But, with options like that, what *was* it that I wanted to do? When I was in kindergarten, I sat inside our black Labrador Duke's wooden dog house looking out at the telephone poles and dreamed of what I would grow up to do for a living. I wanted to climb those telephone poles. Could a girl be a telephone man? I wasn't sure, but liked the possibility.

At that time I wanted to find myself in one of five career choices: to be the first woman to step foot on the moon, to be an attorney, a pilot, a surgeon—or become a waitress. Quite a chasm between them, but the waitresses I was acquainted with were always polite to little kids like me and got to be around my favorite foods.

Dad had a tradition of taking me to Big Boy's on West Main Street for weekend breakfasts of blueberry pancakes with strawberry syrup. My daddy placed such an importance of our being together at our Saturday morning laminate table tops that I felt a deep fondness for being there. And, have I mentioned that I like food? After my grandmother closed her A&W drive-in restaurant (with the best toquitos in town), she opened a Kentucky Fried Chicken eatery that shared a building with my grandpa's Dairy Queen/Burger Mart. I was a master at making sky-high ice-cream cones and dipping them into the flavored topping that would harden in seconds. They also owned a melodrama dinner theater called Wild West Pizza. I didn't know the "wild West" was wild enough to have pizza, but my grandparents sure knew how to dish up great restaurant food. I was sure I could become a great waitress.

I've never had a waitressing job, and I've not been to law school, climbed a telephone pole, or walked on the moon, for that matter. God simply has had other plans for me. But the thought of going somewhere far, far away under this layer of clouds thrilled me.

I was around five-years-old when I first heard about missionaries. I recall sitting in church with my family when the pastor showed the congregation the fundraising chart for a missions organization—founded by a woman—who'd become a missionary in the 1800s! Not only was I awestruck that someone could venture off solo to unknown lands to impact the lives of people who spoke other languages, but that a *woman* in the mid-19th century would do such a thing seemed beyond incredible. I felt challenged.

Where on earth did I want to go? I studied my grandfather's globe as I sat beside it on top of his desk. I loved feeling the cool, smooth paper as it spun beneath my hands, and how each country was colored in old-world shades of sepia brown as if Christopher Columbus himself had penned that particular globe.

When the safari-telling story guy in the wingback chair from Saturday morning cartoons would tell his tales, I was mesmerized and craved to visit the places he talked about through his handlebar moustache, smoky pipe, and gruff southern accent. The animal life enticed me too—I wanted to see a cheetah and the other wild creatures that the African desert held, and people unvisited by Americans seemed to summon my soul. I dreamed of someday doing just as that woman missionary had done. But was leaving everyone you love behind and forsaking everything familiar worth it? Until then, what would I do? I was just a kid and didn't know how to get there.

What *was* my identity? I had at some point entered my sixteenth year, yet I didn't feel any different. I was still waiting for some magic to turn my life into something grand.

CHAPTER 4

The Search Was On

I thought I could find myself in pretending to be others. So back in junior high, I talked myself into trying out for drama class. I supposed that if I learned how other characters thought and behaved, I would somehow acquire skills to be a better "me."

The beauty of the desert Southwest where I grew up lures many Hollywood production companies. The Rocky Mountain region's majesty, colored with such a splendorous contrast of nearby desert hues and sand sculptures, makes for spectacular cinematography. So, with up-close-and-personal experiences in observing the production of several big screen movies, I found myself overcome with the wonder and magic of film and portraying someone else's story.

In addition to my grandma Hill's melodrama dinner theater, my second cousin, playwright Sharon French, also had a melodrama dinner theater. Many in my family are gifted with artistic talent, which blessed me with theater exposure galore.

So, now that I was in high school, I wanted to develop my own acting skills. I threw myself into speech-and-debate club, and drama class and started reading books about why people act the way that they do. The underlying motivation for all of it was that I was on a quest to uncover, or discover, or create— "me."

As a sophomore, when my friend Avery and I were getting ready for the next dance, I was out-of-my-skin excited. We were preparing for self-declared roles at the dance as "punk rockers." I didn't even know what a punk rocker was. She explained that we could "just dress wild," whatever that meant.

For the occasion, my mom unearthed a furry leopard print mini dress she'd worn in the mod 1970s. She still had her brown suede leather boots that came up over the knee—and happened to fit me like a glove. Avery helped me "punk out" my hair, and for the first time, I dared venture away from my usual multipurpose Indian Earth henna powder makeup. This time I packed on dark shades of green eye shadow with thick black eye liner and bright red lipstick. I forced a large safety pin through each of my pierced ear lobes and made a chain of the pins from my left ear to one on the dress. I wasn't sure if I could fit into the punk-rock crowd, or even if I wanted to, but I sure liked the sound of the music when we walked in the door of the darkened school cafeteria.

I didn't know any of the songs playing—I hadn't heard any of them on my Casey Kasem Top-40 albums. The DJ played groups I'd never heard of, like UB-40, Flock of Seagulls, the Talking Heads, Depeche Mode, Modern English, the Circle Jerks, Devo, the B-52s, the Clash, the Ramones, the Dead Kennedy's, the Eurythmics, and the Psychedelic Furs. I connected with the fun bounce and techno sound many of the songs projected—they were notably different from the Donny and Marie style I was used to hearing. I decided I liked punk better than the ballads of Lionel Ritchie and Air Supply. Singing about rock lobsters, running so far away, and doing the Safety Dance was far more fun than singing sappy stuff about being "All Out of Love."

Kids from my old junior high school dances had nothing on these teenagers. For one thing, they were not all hugging the wall, afraid of each other. Everyone was in a big jumping blob in the middle of the floor having a blast, and I wanted in on it. There weren't many other people dressed "punk," so my outfit made quite a splash. The others mostly dressed like the daytime school versions of themselves. The punk-version Kristan hardly came off the dance floor before another senior would ask her to dance. I think the other sophomores were scared of the new chick in the fur.

I was too. Who was I becoming?

After the dance, Avery told me we'd been invited to a senior girl's birthday party. I felt badly that we didn't have a gift, but we got the address and found the house. When we walked in, three things floored me.

For some reason, the house didn't have any furniture. The second thing that hit me was that most everyone was smoking cigarettes—real ones, not the kinds made out of stable bark and Bounty paper towels. Not interested. Lastly, they were drinking beer! And they weren't even twenty-one years old! The senior girl was only turning eighteen, yet she was drinking alcohol! I was panic stricken that the cops would show up at any minute and arrest us all; I didn't want my mug shot to show up in the news with me looking like I was a Sid Vicious groupie.

I said something to Avery, and a guy in a baseball cap standing nearby overheard me, and butted in to our conversation.

"Oh, you don't drink beer? We have some punch for you over here!"

He then led me into the kitchen where a blue Igloo cooler in the middle of the floor was filled with Hawaiian Punch and floating pieces of fruit. Our welcoming host informed us that it was "Jungle Juice" and we could have as much as we wanted. It was the tastiest punch I'd ever had. Not one of my family's birthday parties had juice quite like it.

I was thirsty from all the bouncing and head bobbing I'd done at the dance and quickly chugged three or four cups and downed several bites of fruit. I followed Avery around from group to group in pockets of the house and enjoyed meeting new people.

It wasn't long before I started to feel woozy and sensed my lips going numb. Without realizing that I was not in fact speaking softly—I "whispered" to Avery across the room, "AVERY! I THINK SOMETHING'S WEIRD WITH THIS PUNCH! I THINK THE FRUIT MUST BE BAD!"

Our kind host was still serving in the kitchen and walked over to me where I stood in the furnitureless dining room. He then educated me on how he had made his best batch of Jungle Juice yet; he'd injected a watermelon and oranges with Everclear and let them marinate all week before he added them to the Hawaiian Punch/alcohol mix in the cooler.

I didn't know what Everclear was, nor that it ranks twice as high as vodka on the Richter scale, but I knew whatever it was had to bad. Now it was my brain that was marinating in alcohol, and I realized that for the first time in my life, I was drunk. Learning that a high school kid had exceptional bartending skills frightened me a little. I wanted out of that house, out of my mom's boots, out of her mini dress and into my pajamas.

And, I wanted some Band-Aids on my feet. Most of all I wanted the room to stop spinning.

Avery and I stumbled into her avocado green Ford pickup truck, and she weaved her way all over the road to my place with both of us laughing all the way. We miraculously made it safe and sound to my house—with furniture. Thankfully, my mom and stepdad were asleep when we slipped inside, and Avery and I slept it off.

The next morning I washed off my punk face but not the punk phase. I enjoyed the random way of dressing up for special dances or occasionally throwing on an outfit other than polka dots and ballet flats. I never got into the political and anti-establishment/anti-authoritarian side of punk. I did, however, buy my own Adam and the Ants *Prince Charming* album. I also got a cassette tape by Soft Cell and kept my new music right next to Gloria Gaynor and the Beach Boys on the shelf by my record player.

For the most part, though, I was content with "Surfin' USA" and even Neil Diamond's ballads as I continued my identity quest.

Oscar Wilde's words described me well, "Most people are other people. Their thoughts are someone else's opinions, their lives a mimicry, their passions a quotation."

I was afraid to stand up with my own opinion, and I wasn't even sure if I had opinions of my own—I was ignorant of too much; I still didn't know who I was or who I wanted to be, but I had some great friends and I thought we were having great fun.

CHAPTER 5

Brock McBaggage

One boyfriend I had great fun with was Brock McBaggage.

Would you believe we met in one of my most embarrassing moments ever? Of course. As if all the other embarrassing things I'd done were not a big deal—like when I passed out while giving blood and the time I fell on my face into my leftover pizza box as I crossed the street in front of rush-hour traffic.

While I may have been a good kickball kicker—and often one of the first to be chosen by the kickball team captain—I was as big a clod on the badminton court as I had been at the Sonic Drive-In on my first date. There I was that Friday morning my sophomore year, trying to casually demonstrate outstanding racquet-to-shuttlecock synchronization, but I couldn't concentrate. I didn't even have the finesse it took to win the new video games Pac Man and Asteroids. (Man, I wanted my initials in that winners bracket on the Pac Man screen at Godfather's Pizza on San Juan Boulevard. I was still working on my Atari Pong skills, so I could finally beat my

28

little brother.) Tennis, ping pong, and apparently badminton were not games I could play with any great savviness—and the game in the gym that day was for an actual grade that would affect my grade point average and college entrance! Badminton was fun, but I imagine it would have been a lot more enjoyable if I'd actually been good at it.

Maybe if I wasn't so distracted. For weeks I'd thought that I kept hearing someone shout my name during P.E. class. My teammate Victoria pointed out that it was a couple of upper-class boys who were distracting us with their hollering from the weight room upstairs that overlooked the gym below. I looked forward to going to gym class because I had secret admirers—but perhaps they were merely mocking my lack of athleticism day after day and I was in fact being bullied. I had no idea if the hollering was from some creepy guys or if they would turn out to be people I just might like.

They kept calling my name, nothing else—just "KRISTAN!" in all sorts of different voices, as if I didn't know it was the same two guys hollering every day. I couldn't see them but they could see me, and I felt like a dork in our outdated P.E. uniform. I think the uniforms were the originals that my mom and her classmates had worn twenty years earlier. At least I wasn't the only one wearing the silly-looking faded jumper. I wasn't sure if they'd originally been blue or purple.

At last, that day in March, the two guys made their way down to the drinking fountain near the court where I was making an attempt to finally score. As I drew back my racquet and swung with all my might to hit that blasted birdie over the net, somehow inertia swept in behind the racquet and I got a quick object lesson in the law of physics. The racquet itself escaped my sweaty hand and went soaring through the air—*smack!*

Right into Brock McBaggage—one of the handsome mystery men who had been shouting my name all those weeks. The dude had finally mustered up enough courage to go beyond calling my name and move in for a closer look—but got a surprise opportunity for a concussion instead.

Too bad I wasn't getting points in the P.E. grade book for having the most embarrassing moments; I'd have been the one who set the bell curve on that subject. There were plenty of embarrassing moments just from our square-dancing segment that would've ranked in the top five.

This embarrassing moment was different.

Brock coolly left his eyes locked onto mine as he bent to retrieve my weapon from the floor—and I was smitten. What is it with guys eye-locking you? Wow.

He waited for me after P.E. that day to walk me to my next class, then took me to lunch. At the stroke of noon, he did not turn into an octopus. He did not tell me, "I love you." He was just easy to be with. He was comfortable and fit me better than my mom's suede high-top boots. His glimmering yellow car in the parking lot was even better than Brunette Barbie's convertible (mostly because his car was not constructed out of cheap plastic, the doors indeed opened and the axles remained intact around corners). We became inseparable.

CHAPTER 6

I Lost It

In the year we dated leading up to the point I'm about to tell you, Brock never equaled Mark's red roses in the grass romance quotient. He simply wasn't the sensitive type.

When he wasn't working and I wasn't busy practicing for a play or a dance recital or traveling to a speech tournament, we'd go to an occasional movie, ride horses, or hang out with other couples. We went to parties with other friends from school and started drinking alcohol—on purpose, not like I had done by accident at the furnitureless house. Brock was nice and had a lot of friends that I liked being around. He was a great guy—just not the sensitive, romantic type.

But Brock was saving his money for college. He had a large goal for his life and I respected his financial conservatism, so if we were not at a party at someone else's house, we would hang out at either of our homes with our parents. We went for drives in the countryside and visited other people, but we didn't have that much to do together. I liked being with him; it was easy. We didn't go to a lot of movies or out to eat much. We were actually kind of boring, I guess, which probably helped get us into trouble later on. Maybe if we'd been on a city volleyball league or Frisbee team, a chess club (gag) or—heck even a badminton team—anything to give us something to *do*, it would have been better.

But I'll get to that soon.

While he was not the flowers, sunsets, and sparklers kind of guy, I enjoyed being with him and we shared the same faith.

Believing in God was important to me. Grandmama Griffith had taught me the books of the Bible when I was in first grade, and I loved hearing her tell Bible stories and learning about this Jesus she spoke about in such a personal way. To this day I still have the bookmarker that I made in Sunday school when I was six. It references Isaiah 40:8, which says, *"The grass withers and the flowers fade, but the word of our God stands forever"* (New Living Translation).

I didn't really know what *else* the "word of our God" said—but I knew that whatever it said it would always be there—unchanging—something I could stand firm on, no matter what storm of life would come my way. That gave me great comfort. The Holy Spirit had embossed that verse onto my heart. However, at the tender of age of six when I memorized those words, I didn't know that I would someday cling to them—for dear life.

Brock's parents were as active in their church as a couple can be. I was glad that I went to Sunday school with Brock and to the youth group that would meet in a different teenager's home each Friday night. It was nice to know there were other students out there who believed in Jesus too.

Our relationship hit a dry place, though. After we had been dating for a long time, it seemed like sex was just the next thing we were "supposed" to do, regardless of whether or not we were Christians. Even some who I respected called me "old fashioned" because I was a virgin. I was not comfortable with the idea of having sex, but I was curious.

I don't even remember our first kiss. I should, but I don't. We started kissing a lot. That became our activity. I do, however, vividly remember everything about the first time that we had sex.

That old childhood peer pressure to smoke, to kiss and to sneak into the candy store came flooding back. Why didn't I say "no" back then, and, dear God in heaven, why didn't I say no to Brock?

It was the first week in December when we went to his house for lunch; it was a Thursday. We only had about forty minutes before we had to be back for our next class. No one else was home. Brock led me into his room. Big mistake. The biggest mistake of my life. Things moved quickly from the time we started kissing. I encourage other kids now—the first time you kiss someone should be when the pastor says, "You may now kiss the bride," because once you start that train, it sure is difficult to stop it.

We had not planned for our first time to have sex to be during lunch—nor did we plan to have it at his house. We didn't talk about it in the slightest bit. We didn't have any sort of plan ... at least I didn't think so. I was surprised when Brock pulled a condom from his pocket. I didn't even know he had one and couldn't imagine where he had gotten it. He apparently did have a plan and I followed his lead.

After some intimate time—the condom broke. It just broke.

I didn't think it was a big deal, but Brock utterly freaked out. He wasn't angry—he was terrified. He immediately panicked, "I know you're pregnant!"

He was beside himself and hurriedly threw his jeans on and rushed to get us out of the house before what we had done was uncovered by anyone.

I kept telling him, "But it's our first time! It's the first time I have *ever* had sex! I can't be pregnant! We hardly even did anything! It was too quick! Don't worry!"

He would not leave it alone.

He apparently had planned on having sex since he had been prepared with "protection," but he had not planned beyond that … nor had I.

We had to rush back to school to get there on time. I slipped into my seat against the blackboard in English class, and as I leaned against the cold, sharp eraser tray, I lost everything the teacher was saying. My classmates blurred and my teacher's voice droned on. I couldn't believe I had just lost my virginity … during lunchtime no less, not on my wedding night. Not after a romantic evening or on a cruise ship or in a swanky hotel on an exotic Caribbean island honeymoon. I was in high school—and we did it at his house during a short lunch break from school! What ever happened to my little-girl dreams? It was nothing like I thought it should have been.

I played the scenario over and over and over in my head. I lost my virginity and understood why they call it "losing" it. I felt like I had just lost a very big part of whoever I was. A huge piece of my soul felt brutally extracted, even though Brock had not raped me. I just knew something was missing. I was different. I loved him, I really did and I wanted a future with him—but I was afraid. My innocence was forever gone.

The girl in the seat in front of me broke through the fog and asked if I was OK. I looked into her worried eyes, but all I could muster was a slow, faint, "I lost it."

"What did you lose?" she asked.

Shaking my head, I repeated, "I lost it … I just lost it." She may have figured out what I meant, I don't know, the thick fog closed in again and the next thing I knew the bell was ringing, pressuring me to get up out of my seat and move on to the next class. Life was moving on that simply.

Tick, tock.

In my next class, I watched the red second hand on the big black-and-white clock slam past every mark like spankings. I felt such shame and fear of what was going to happen next in my life. How could I go home to my family and sit at the dinner table like nothing had changed? Something mammoth had happened that day.

Dinner consisted of a moist Crock-Pot roast with potatoes and carrots, a side salad, peas, bread and butter with iced tea and a super-sized serving of guilt. My parents retired to the den to watch TV while my brother went into his room and I excused myself quickly to my own sanctuary in the house.

I had to talk to someone, so I phoned a friend who'd be in the know and divulged everything that had happened that day.

"I'll take you to a clinic and they can tell you what you need to know," she said calmly.

She told she'd take me there the next week—I wouldn't even have to tell my parents anything.

I called Brock and tried to reassure him, "I will go to the doctor and find out that everything is fine, and I'll get on the pill so we don't have to worry about it again."

He wasn't convinced. He whimpered, "I know you're pregnant. I just know it."

I didn't believe him—how could I be? After some small talk, we hung up the phone and I somehow found sleep.

Lunch time again. This day was powerfully different than the one before. My caring friend drove me to the treatment center, and I was comforted that she knew the woman working there. I told the tall slender expert what had happened and she asked some very personal questions I did not want to answer.

She asked, "When was your last period?"

"Oh, everything's fine … it's been around two weeks since my last cycle—I'm only here to get on the pill," I countered.

The hesitation and drop in her tone brought alarm to all my senses, and I listened intently as she explained the facts of life. I had not paid attention in biology class! All I remember, besides the art of dissecting frogs and their accompanying stench, was being jealous of how pretty Georgia Droycovich was.

Teenage pregnancy would never happen to me, right?

The clinician urged me to come back in several days because a pregnancy test during the initial visit could not be accurate so soon after conception. I did return for the test, still confident that everything was going to be fine and I could get the birth control I needed the next time I was there. We left and I tried to put it all out of my mind.

A few days or so later, I stood staring at the pay phone on the pole in The Quad at the center of our school. I had to muster up the guts to make that call to the clinic and find out what the future held in store for me. Would life go on like normal, or was I going to hang up the dull-gray, hard-plastic phone with very cold and very hard facts?

The woman on the other end spoke with a clinical tone; she sounded like one of those automated telemarketing calls, but, oh, I heard her loud and clear. She said frankly, "The test came back positive. You are pregnant."

I looked down at my burgundy A-line skirt with the thick black elastic waistband and thought about how much I liked the fabric's sheen and my coordinating black Bolero jacket with oversized buttons. I especially liked my black leather Mary Jane pump shoes and the way they looked with my printed pantyhose, kind of tap-dance style—kind of old Hollywood. My hair was in a chic up-do with a few wisps left down to frame my face. I felt "put together" in the ensemble—and I felt very, very, *very* old. I felt like I was thirty-seven. Where did my 'sweet sixteen and never been kissed' fantasy go? *What had I done?*

I asked the all-knowing Oz on the other end of the phone what my next move was, and she told me that I had to wait six weeks from conception before I could have an abortion.

She paused and asked, "What do you want to do?"

I *wanted* to run away. I *wanted* to go back to kickball when things were sure and the hardest things I had to process were multiplication tables and figure out how to do them backward and call it division. I *wanted* to "Make the World Go Away."[5]

For the first time, I took a surveyor's look at my school and saw nothing but concrete, brick, and metal that boxed me in. Everyone else who had been rushing past me that December day was going on with their lives. The Quad cleared. Winter's sting attached itself to the news in my ears and bound my mind, my heart and my body. I stood alone in the silent sterile courtyard … I was learning something dramatically different than I'd ever imagined there at my school that day.

"I'll get back with you," I told her, and hung up the phone as the final bell rang, reminding me I had another class.

Tick, tock.

What *was* I going to do? I could move to another state and live with my dad, stepmom, and other siblings; but I didn't want to move away from my mom, stepdad, and younger brother. I had been "the new girl" at this school and it wasn't so bad, but if I moved to a new place as "the *pregnant* new girl," I was sure to be an outcast. I imagined a cold and clammy village in seventeenth century Boston with overgrown vegetation and a big scarlet letter on my chest. I might as well have shown up at school in a red suit with horns and a tail, carrying a pitch fork. I speculated how challenging it might be to hide a baby under my clothes without drawing suspicion: I had a small waist, so surely a basketball bulge could be hidden. Maybe I could trade my A-line skirts with thick belts for outfits with empire waistlines—and no one would know.

No one could know.

Brock echoed the sentiment, insisting with great passion that *no one could know!* After all, there were family members who held important church positions and it would embarrass them. I argued with him that it was a *baby* and how could we *kill* the very life we had created? He debated back with "scientific" and "medical" phrases that swapped the label of "baby" to "fetus." He went on to reason that it was OK to abort "it," because "it" was just a "mass." I wondered what he meant by "mass"—wasn't that a term they used for a church service? Or cancer? Clearly I understood that a baby was not a cancer to be cut out, but he was telling me that at six weeks "old," the "fetus" was a "mass."

I studied more on the subject—it wasn't hard to find material even in the days before the Internet started bringing instant knowledge to our fingertips. After all, the TV news and papers were screaming about this blistering social and moral debate, showing graphic pictures and angry picketers on both sides of the issue. There was so much that I did not understand. I was in way over my head—I was still a kid.

My world-wise education came abruptly. The earliest an abortion could be performed was at six weeks gestation when the baby was forming a heart and blood was beginning to flow through the "mass," creating veins.

I thought about that—blood flowing through the embryo at six weeks and I was going to medically stop that process so no more blood could flow, no more baby would grow, and I could go on my merry way. It would be as if nothing had ever happened and no one would know any differently.

Confusion and fear swarmed my mind like a nest of bees on fire, and Brock was horrified of what might happen if I did *not* abort the baby. Would our lives be over if I did *not* have an abortion?

He pressured me until I gave in. I didn't know what else to do—it seemed like the only way out. I loved all four of my parents and each of my grandparents so much, and I felt that I couldn't let them down. I believed that all my family members would have been so disappointed in me for getting pregnant before I was married, and I just couldn't bring myself to tell them.

In the seventh grade I had changed a report card's F into a B with a nice cover-up. Although I had gotten caught then, maybe this would be a cover-up I could get away with. I knew that a medical procedure and scandal like this would be far more challenging to hide than smudging a penned letter on a report card, but I could think of no better way out. How could I shame my boyfriend's family? How could I shame my family? No, I had to act fast. Whatever that thing was called inside me, it was growing by the minute.

We finally planned something. Brock would drive me sixty minutes to the nearest abortion clinic over the state line, and he would pay the two hundred dollar fee. Two hundred bucks and my life would belong solely to me again. That was all it would cost.

Or was it?

We had to schedule it soon. I looked at the calendar. The six-week mark of when I should have the abortion fell only a couple of days before *my seventeenth birthday.*

The clinic would not do it any earlier, and I didn't want to wait any longer … at what point did the "mass" become a human? The debate was still raging and I did not know what to think. I was not comfortable with it any way I looked at it.

Sweet seventeen and my boyfriend was buying me an abortion for my birthday.

No long-stemmed roses, no romantic sunset.

No sparklers.

No Purple Cow.

Not even a goat.

An abortion.

And no one could know.

Oh, I'm sure Brock bought me a necklace or something, but he was spending two hundred dollars of his hard-earned money on "fixing" what we'd done wrong, and he paid for the gasoline to get us to the clinic and back. My birthday just happened to fall at a bad time—everything was all out of order. Perhaps an abortion would set everything right.

CHAPTER 7

Terminated

The next weeks spent waiting for the dreaded drive were harsh, to say the least. I could not sleep, could not concentrate on schoolwork, and nothing could take my mind off of the changes I felt happening inside my body—and in my heart. I was supposed to be a kid in the prime of my youth but that was all gone. My life would never hold the same innocent perspective. Now that I had crossed that threshold from being a sexually innocent virgin, there was no going back—especially now that I was pregnant.

The day came to do the deed, and as it always does during the week of my January 16th birthday, it snowed. This time, instead of being thrilled with all the outdoor opportunities the powdery mix offered, it served only as a reminder that winter is a season of death and icy dreary overcast days which left me shivering in the dark.

I met Brock in the school parking lot at eight o'clock, right on schedule. I would be back at the school by midafternoon. If anyone asked why I'd missed class, I would simply lie and say something like I had overslept or that I had gone to the dentist.

Thankfully, no one asked, so I could stay quiet … no one would know … anything.

We had been on the road for about thirty minutes when we saw red and blue flashing lights behind us. Brock was in a hurry to reach our appointment and get it all over with, but the police officer did not see fit to let our speeding car get away with a warning.

I imagined the cop letting us off with an understanding nod if he knew *why* we needed to get to our destination quickly. If only he would say something like, "Oh, you're pregnant and are going to get an abortion? No one can know? Of course you should get there immediately. I'll escort you!"

Where had this officer of the peace who'd sworn "to serve and protect" been that day in Brock's bedroom? I felt out of control yet was relieved that there was someone out there still setting boundaries and intending to look after the public's best interest. Was an abortion *really* in my best interest? In Brock's? How was an abortion going to affect him?

We got a ticket. It felt more like a warning that we should turn around, go back home, and leave our foolish idea in the gutter on the side of the road where it belonged.

Nine o'clock. It was time. The small clinic waiting room was unwelcoming. The staff spoke frankly like I was at their window to order an assembly-line burger with scant ketchup disproportionately placed off the edge of the beef. No one asked if I wanted a large bag of fries and a chocolate shake.

I was hungry but wasn't supposed to eat before the procedure. I filled out a short form and waited my turn. When I heard them call my name, I remember hearing it differently—as if "Kristan" were someone else in the lobby. It could not be *me* they wanted to go into the mysterious back room. Generally when someone called me by name, it was with light-hearted fun or to invite me to join them in whatever great activity they were involved in. Or, because they just wanted to spend time to be with me. Not this.

I heard my name called again.

Brock's calling, "Kristan" in the gym months ago echoed in my mind.

I stood up and turned to look at Brock. He stayed planted in the waiting room, his heels dug in deep under the chair. I would need someone to drive me home afterward, but he did not want to be in the room with me when it happened. Maybe he didn't get a choice, I don't know. I just remember looking back at him as I walked through the door and being petrified about what was about to happen. My mom had always accompanied my every medical, dental, or orthodontist appointment. This was new. I was completely alone for the biggest medical procedure of my life.

I felt wholly isolated in this new side of the medical community that seemed like a black-and-white 1960s science fiction flick. Where was the film crew? The lights and cameras were nowhere in sight. This was really happening. It was all one hundred percent real, and it was happening to *me*. A veil had been lifted and I saw the world differently from that day on.

I slipped into one of the ridiculous gowns the medical community degrades us all with and gingerly climbed onto the exam table. How did they come up with the name "gown" for that thing, anyway? What about it fits its name? The fabric? Uh, no, I can't imagine a Vera Wang gown looking anything like that. Is it the wrap design? Maybe Target or Wal-Mart could have this item amongst their disposable clothing section for ninety-nine cents. I think it would be better named "Sheath of Shame" or "So-wrong Sarong," don't you? I suppose the medical marketing community wants to class up the nasty thing as best they can by giving it a moniker like "gown." They would never sell those frocks at Dillard's. My Barbies had better gowns than this.

There I sat in my drafty So-wrong Sarong trying to think of anything else besides what was coming. I'd never felt more vulnerable ... like a sheep being prepared for slaughter.

A nurse came in and the doctor followed. At their direction, I edged back and put my head on the thin pillow case wrapped around a slight wad of stuffing. Apparently they didn't want anyone getting too comfortable. My eyes landed on a small poster of a mountain range that was taped to the ceiling. I remembered seeing a similar poster in my grade-school book order form and wished I could click my heels together three times and wake up inside the poster in a different realm.

I slipped my socked feet into the stirrups. The cotton did nothing to keep out the bite of the cold metal. A woman, who I assume was a nurse, wheeled a cart with a machine sitting on top of it closer to my side as the doctor made small talk about the poster he noticed me eyeing.

The doctor verbally repeated the procedure that had been explained to me in the first clinic—so that I would be "more relaxed," knowing what to expect. I was well aware that there was no putting me to sleep for the procedure; I would be oh-so-wide awake. The nurse flipped on the power button to the extraction machine. It sounded like a vacuum cleaner.

He changed the subject back to the poster and wished he'd shut up as he worked. He was not fooling me with trying to drown out the sound of the machine with his voice, and he certainly was not easing any of the sharp pains I felt inside my no-longer-private areas. I could not bring myself to answer any more of his shallow questions—my lips were beginning to quiver and my eyes were welling up with tears as the heavy bowling-ball-sized lump in my throat began to claim my oxygen intake. I coughed, trying to loosen the weighted ball; it only made the pain below all the more intense.

If the doctor cared about me or my situation, why didn't he ask me anything real? What about my soul that was deeply distraught? Was what he was doing to my body truly helping me? It was my choice to do what I wanted with my body, but what about the body that was being formed inside my womb? It did not seem fair that that tiny person did not get to make a choice whether to live or die. Did that "insignificant" thing have a spirit inside? Why shouldn't he or she get a choice? At what point does the "mass" gain a soul? I deliberated more, wondering if it was the other way around. Was it a soul or spirit first, then it gained a body? I didn't dare think on the subject any further. I forced back my stomach that tried to sneak past my tonsils, wiped more tears, and listened to the doctor mumble on about his hobbies.

How nice for him.

I wish I had not seen what I saw. It was an accident. I had tried hard not to look. They tried to keep things concealed— much in the way I was concealing the fact that I was—had been—pregnant. But I saw things that no one should *ever*, in any way, see. No one. Not even doctors or nurses themselves should see what was in that room.

I thought I remembered reading somewhere that when healthcare professionals become official caretakers, they take the Hippocratic Oath whereby they swear something to the effect of, "I will not give a deadly drug to anybody if asked for it, nor will I make such a suggestion. I will not give to a woman an abortive remedy. In purity and holiness I will guard my life and my art." I must have been wrong. I had to be wrong. Everything felt—very—wrong. *Hippocratic* ... is that where we get the word *hypocrite*? I felt like the embodiment of the word because there I was feeling like what I was doing was wrong, yet I was going through with it anyway. I pushed the thoughts out of my mind again and reasoned with myself that this was the only way out.

The doctor was finished almost as soon as he had begun. I thought it would have taken a whole lot longer, but that was it. Now my life would be mine again and Brock's life would be his. Any obligation he may have had was now fulfilled by *my* yielding *my* body to the man in the white coat and the chugging vacuum.

The nurse-lady-person led me and my wobbling legs around a corner to a post-op room. I noted that there were many other women in there—I didn't want to make eye contact with anyone, so I buried my chin on my chest. Why was I suddenly not alone anymore? Especially now I wanted to be left completely alone—I did not want strangers looking at me. Everything within me hurt like I had the flu; every layer of skin and muscle tissue felt heavy and like it was slipping off of my skeleton. My female parts particularly hurt with searing pains—my heart felt even worse.

The medical professional told me to lie down in one of the short, narrow reclining chairs. The problem was, the only empty seat happened to be next to a host of other women who, I assumed by their somber behavior, were there for the same reason I was. It looked like a row of beach resort lounge chairs where we should all be sipping cool tropical drinks with little umbrellas poking out the top and passing sunscreen to each other. I thought this event was supposed to be discreet so that "no one could know."

How on earth had a dozen or so of us gotten pregnant unexpectedly? Why so many? Were condoms that fragile? Would there be more groups flowing through the building throughout the day or was this particular morning an infrequent occurrence? I was flabbergasted that there were so many of us. How many abortions did that one clinic perform that one January day? Were there other doctors in that one town doing this on the same day—or oh my word—*every* day? How many of us were there, anyway? How many could there be in my state—and in the United States? What about in other countries? A soft *wow*, almost fell out of my mouth as I realized the possible enormity of what was happening, but I wasn't about to be the one to break the heavy silence in our "beach club."

I took my place in the lineup without even speaking to the nurse.

She handed me a pill and a small blue-and-yellow-flowered Dixie cup only half filled with water and said, "Here. It's Valium to help you relax."

I didn't hear if she said anything else.

Hmm … Valium … something to treat anxiety. My heart felt like it had just been "terminated" as well. Was that little tablet supposed to calm my mind too? Relax-schmelax! I had just done the most dramatic thing in my life and I was supposed to be calm about it? That was it? "Here's a pill—it's all 'over' now"? Where was the hard stuff? I wanted to find a phlebotomist from the American Red Cross blood mobile, get his rubber hose to wrap around my bicep, and shoot my vein with something that would really knock me out. But here I was in silent group "recovery" with everyone preparing to step out that door and go on with their lives. How could I "terminate" my thoughts? How long was long enough to gain a full recovery anyway?

Tick, tock.

I stayed in the post-op room for what they deemed was "long enough" before a woman led me back to Brock and sent me on my way.

The drive back was pretty. I love winterscapes, and I asked Brock to please pull over to let me play in the snow for a little bit. I just was not quite ready to go back to school and face everyone. I needed time to prepare for the greatest acting role of my life. I had to act "normal," and needed time to "develop my character."

Brock complained that he had to get me back to class and he had to go to work, but I begged to get out of the car. Was I nauseous from the Valium, the procedure, or from vertigo created by my mind reeling off of its axis? Whatever it was—I needed air. He bucked my request but pulled over anyway.

I was still not used to the idea that I'd recently lost my virginity; I'd also just lost a baby that lived in what should have been a safe sanctuary in the warmth of my body. On top of that, I was supposed to be celebrating my *birthday*, not experiencing the worst horror I'd ever experienced in my life.

The cold mountain air felt refreshing on my face as I stepped off the side of the road. He kept the car engine running while waiting for me to play in the snow on the side of the road alone. I stepped into the beautiful white fluff that seemed welcoming and safe and quickly sunk into it up to my hips. I felt the snow promptly begin to melt next to my skin inside my boots. I thought about leaning back and falling into the soft ground cover and making a snow angel, but I'd been given instructions not to be active for a while and to call with any excessive bleeding.

I found myself again caring about what others thought of me. How weird would it look to those driving by if they were to see a girl making snow angels in the snow on the shoulder of a busy highway? Hmm … were there any angels out there along that highway that day?

My snowy moment of calm was cut short when I heard Brock shout from his warm seat, "Are you about done playing?"

He was concerned about my physical health, "Remember what they said!" he warned.

My body was in pain and I longed to be free again. I was playing there in the mountains that held my secret and yearned to be farther off road and much farther away from the current world that I knew. I coveted the idea of really "playing" and being carefree again. I stood there stuck in the quick-sand-like stuff, watching the vehicles whiz past on the road and staring at the curious passersby. I wished I could have climbed in with any one of them heading north and left everything I knew behind.

His car horn startled me.

I shuttered with reality that snaked up my spine, over the top of my cold head, then turned and stared me square in the eyes; its slithering mocking tongue spit fear in my face.

A deep breath of the mountain air filled my lungs, and I burned to hold in its freshness until it seeped into my brain and heart.

Back in the car headed south, I heard objections of getting his carpet dirty with soot from the road and plowed snow.

My lungs demanded another breath, my nostrils flared, and I exhaled as slowly as I could, clinging to every ounce of the mountain air as if I were letting go of my very last breath on earth. The replacement air I'd captured outside dissipated into his foggy windshield.

My growling stomach reminded me I'd not yet eaten anything.

"Can we stop somewhere and get something to eat?" I asked softly.

He marked our remaining time before he had to get me back to school, and he had to be at work shortly after lunch. We made time for a stop at a fast-food joint. I could get that assembly-line burger—and a chocolate shake, but I wasn't ravenously hungry, I just needed something to calm my gut.

We made pointless small talk, and what we talked about during the hour drive back, I don't know. I have no idea what was going on in his head. Was he relieved? I'm sure. Had this affected him emotionally at all, or was it just like he'd taken me to get my teeth cleaned? Was he experiencing any grieving for the loss of life? Did he have any more concerns, or had they all been addressed in the clinic? He had not wanted me to jump around in the snow, but he didn't chase me down to pull me out. That would have been nice—I would have felt rescued in some way. Having him chase me was certainly not my motive for getting out of the car; I had just needed an immediate escape. But I did feel like I needed rescuing and he was the sitting "knight in shining armor." I don't remember knowing what he was thinking and don't recall asking—I was quite consumed with thoughts of my own. He must have been too.

The one hour drive back to our town seemed to take forever … a lifetime. Mile after mile I watched the white line zoom past on the ground outside my window. Dejected, I watched my beloved mountain range diminish into the distance, and saw the words etched as a caption in the mirror reflecting them, "Objects in mirror are closer than they appear." They grew smaller and farther away, only reminding me that what I was seeing was a fake image. I was being mocked. Nothing from that point on could be real. I longed deeply for my favorite place of real peace back in the mountain range—but it was untouchable, unattainable from the mile marker where I was. How long would that be the case for my life? Was tranquility as far gone from me as my virginity? I felt totally and completely lost.

I looked at the clock on the dashboard and dreaded having to go back to school where I would have to act like the most monolithic event in my life had never happened. I leaned my head against the foggy car window and cleared a spot to see that white boundary line that separated the highway lane from the shoulder of the road.

Several more miles clicked by.

I slowly unlocked the door and put my hand back in my lap. I looked out again—the boundary was still there, guiding our way.

I put my hand on the chrome-plated door handle and wondered how far over the line I could jump. I contemplated how to manipulate my footing so I could propel my body far enough away from the car to clear the back tire. How close could I roll to the edge of the cliff at sixty miles per hour? Would I die if I jumped? It seemed like it would be a quick death albeit a painful one.

We drove for many more miles with my hand still on the door handle. I'd seen actors in movies jump out of speeding vehicles or trains, dust themselves off, and go on their merry way. But I'd also seen the making of too many movies, and had seen too many cowboys dumped off of their bucking animals. I knew firsthand how badly stunt men and bull riders get messed up with wounds they often carry the rest of their lives. Was I going to let my aversion to pain stop me from jumping out of the car? I was already in pain and didn't like the idea of any more. If I jumped, I wanted to make sure I'd be dead. No hospital time for me—just straight to the morgue. I wanted nothing more to do with doctors or nurses.

The hypnotic motion and hum of the road kept rhythm with the static songs on the radio. I looked at my right hand back on the lever, then leaned my head onto my left hand and twirled my hair.

If I did jump, Brock could just keep driving and say he didn't see a thing. I don't think he saw my hand on the handle. He couldn't possibly know that I was considering taking a leap out of his vehicle.

I could not imagine what it would feel like to hit the pavement or to get whipped by the brush on the side of the road before my body came to a stop, but what a temptation it was! If only I could just be gone in the blink of an eye and wake up in heaven with the baby I'd left in pieces back at the clinic. I didn't want to land in the hospital with a failed attempt of suicide—that would be terrible. I didn't necessarily want to die right then. I just didn't want to have my life as I knew it. How could it be real? Had I really had an *abortion*?

I pulled my hand back into my lap, then held it with my other hand. I could feel the pulse in my fingertips and looked down to see that I was holding hands with myself. I grabbed Brock's hand beside me, and we stayed touching like that without saying anything for a long time.

The white line on the roadside stopped at the school, and I quietly blended back into the crowded hallway as classes were changing.

Brock was on time to clock in at work.

No one knew our day had been anything other than routine.

No one could know.

CHAPTER 8

They Knew

My seventeenth birthday celebration came and left without much fanfare, and I was thankful there was neither a big surprise party nor a rented hall for a large list of guests. The day was purely highlighted by the traditional homemade German chocolate cake and ice cream with extended family. I couldn't help but think about that gold watch I'd gotten for my previous birthday; I certainly didn't feel like I could wear it anymore.

Although Mom knew I'd been kissed, I don't know that she had any idea anything further had happened since then. I was not about to tell her.

But it wasn't long before our deep dark secret came to light.

One morning I was getting ready in my bathroom adjacent to my room when Mom came in and sat down on my water bed. We had a little conversation and apparently I answered her sharply.

She asked, "Why have you been such a b– lately? Are you on the pill?"

I was stunned at her language and realized that my behavior must have been quite rude since she was speaking to me in a way she never had before. For the life of me, I could not think of a specific conversation or event that would have made her clash with me like this. I must have just been being quite a grouch overall. I felt badly that I'd somehow offended her and had no clue how to answer. Why *was* I coming across in such an awful way? I felt that I had every reason to be, but how could I tell her? I was tired of acting "normal." Clearly I was not about to win any academy awards.

My silent stone face angered her all the more, and she raised her voice, demanding answers. She shouted her interrogation this time, *"Are you on the pill?* WHAT'S WRONG WITH YOU?"

I had to answer her; I was now cornered in the bathroom. I squared my shoulders and stood eye to eye—not wanting to hurt her—but grateful that someone I knew truly cared for me and was finally rolling up their sleeves to get into my messy, putrid business.

I simply said "No, I'm not on the pill ...," I paused to be sure I wanted the truth to fall out of my mouth. "... I ... had an abortion."

I said it. There it was, and there was no taking it back—for real or in that conversation.

Her reaction was astounding. Her face opened wide with shock, and she hurled herself back hard onto my bed, flailing her arms and feet around, pounding my bed with her fists, and screaming, "NO! NO! NO! NO!"

She wailed a dreadfully awful cry that I had so longed to let loose from my own heart. It sounded pathetic and deep like it came from the inside of her very bones.

I stood there watching her for what seemed like hours. I just stood there watching her crying deplorably, and the more she pounded my water bed, the more violent its waves rolled underneath her.

It was too much for me to take in. Were her dreadful sobs born out of the shock that I was no longer a virgin? Was it the blow that her first grandchild was dead before she could even meet him or her? Did she feel sorry for me? Did she hate me? Was she going to kill me like I had taken the life of my own child? For a second I wished she *would* kill me, so I could stop pretending and be in heaven where there are no more tears or sorrow and it would *all* be over.

I didn't quiz, and she didn't talk—she just cried hysterically. She finally stopped at some point and, much to my amazement, we embraced. Mom is normally a most loving person. If you ever need a hug, you want one from her because she is so comforting and warm, and you know that she truly cares about you. I know now that her cries were out of sheer agony. My mother hurt for me, and the outrageous and emotional news absolutely overtook her—spirit, soul, and body.

I don't remember what happened after my bathroom encounter with my mom. I never talked to my stepdad about it, nor my dad, or even my stepmom for that matter. We simply did not talk about it.

No one could know. That's how it was.

But the next people to find out were the ones we *really wanted to hide it from*: Brock's parents. He called and said, "My mom found the clinic's receipt in the pocket of my jeans when she was doing laundry."

I was furious! How on *earth* could he have pressured me like he did for the *reason* that he did yet be so careless as to leave the receipt where the very person from whom we were hiding our predicament could find it? How *could* he? Dear God, what had we done and how in the world could we ever find normalcy again?

That Sunday before church started, Brock's mom approached me like she was now the one with a secret. I was utterly and completely terrified.

What she said was beyond my comprehension. Of all the gall—how could this woman have such guts to ask me to do such a thing at such a time as this? I was beyond dumbfounded by her way of "handling the situation." I wanted to slap her for it, but I was frozen mannequin-stiff with no sign of life left in me at all. I couldn't move. I was the one left with a much harsher "slap" to the face and was stabbed deep, deep into my heart by her plan—she assigned me to work in the newborn nursery and swiftly led me to a baby awaiting a diaper change.

I thought my heart had already known the most piercing pain a human heart can endure, but she pushed it to the very core of what felt like hell—right there in church.

She towered over me with her tall frame and high heels, and I looked at my new prison warden with nothing to say. I was in absolute shock, still hurting from the procedure and had no words within me for her—I felt only pain in every part of my being. I felt like I was being abused. I was immobilized. She spun around on her heels and left me there alone in the nursery with a beautiful blond baby boy demanding my attention.

She may have known about what happened, but didn't she know that the fear of *her reaction* was one of the major reasons for the decision? Didn't she know that it was *her* son who pushed me to do this because of what *she* and *her* husband and the church peers might have thought? Of course they weren't the only ones whose reactions we considered, but they were the key ingredients. What would my Jesus-loving grandmother have done if she'd have known I'd lost my virginity—and worse?

I don't know how I got through the next hour without crying like a baby myself. There I was in church and I could not even pray.

CHAPTER 9

The Issue of Rape

Some who are against abortion still hold that it should be reserved for rape victims. A *New York Times* report shows that only *one percent* of those who have had an abortion reported that they were victims of rape.[6] One percent. One.

Isn't it interesting, then, that the number of abortions in our nation is equivalent to the wiping out of the population of a small town every day?

I was a victim of rape.

After going through an abortion with Brock, whom I loved very much, I would never have an abortion again—even though I was raped by another person later. Thank God that my rape did not result in pregnancy. Even if it had, though, I would *not* have had another abortion—no matter the circumstance. I would have perhaps given the baby up for adoption. One abortion was beyond more than enough for me.

The rape occurred after Brock and I broke up.

The months after our big drama were ... weird. I was scared speechless around his parents and didn't want to ever go to his house again, but we did. We had to act like nothing had happened.

He soon graduated and moved away to college, and our long-distance relationship proved to be something I wasn't good at holding together. The longer he was away, the more time I had to think about everything. I realized I had been holding on to him because of what we'd gone through. It wasn't a relationship that I wanted to keep forever anymore, even though I truly cared for him. He really was a good guy. I'm sure he is a good husband and father today, and I wish him all the best in the world. It's just time for me to tell this story so that maybe one baby can be saved. Perhaps one more woman who has experienced an abortion will find solace. It may be a longshot, but maybe someone, man or woman, who is involved in the abortion industry, will decide to stop—if I come out with my story.

Here's a question: what if your dad committed a crime, yet *you* were the one who was put to death because of the act *he* committed?

Many American fathers have spent time in jail—how wrong would it be for the courts to take the man's child and lock him or her away instead? Isn't that what we do when we abort babies because of the rape crimes of their fathers?

Of course women who carry babies conceived in rape have a tremendous, constant, reminder … but how can rape rationalize killing?

From my personal experience, I feel strongly that there is *never* a case in which a baby's life should be taken because of the father. Be it rape or incest, I think innocent life should be protected. It's a life. It's a baby—a person. And that person is alive.

When I was raped in 1984, near the end of my senior year of high school, I had a large group of friends and was involved in various school clubs and activities. One night after a school-related function out of town, I was hanging out with classmates in the hotel and we were drinking Jim Beam and Coke. We had a fifth of the whiskey to share between a few of us and set out to get drunk.

There are a lot of things that people do when under the influence that they would never in a million years do when sober.

Throughout the night one of my "friends" kept pouring more and more whiskey into my Coke without my knowledge. So with every drink I took, the alcohol ratio grew more concentrated; and in a short time span, I passed out stone cold from alcohol poisoning.

I remember waking up once that night hanging over the toilet seat, throwing up everything I'd put into my stomach. I was "bowing to the porcelain toilet god," or "driving the porcelain bus," as we used to say. Then I passed out again.

The next thing I knew, I woke up in a separate bedroom with that particular "friend" in the act of raping me. He knew he never would have had my permission to have sex with him otherwise. Ever.

I awoke with extreme panic to find what was happening and sobbed and pleaded with him to make sure he was using a condom so that I wouldn't get pregnant again—he wasn't ... I don't think, anyway. Not like I had a lot of faith in the power of a condom, mind you, it was just the first thing to come to my drunken and shocked mind. I felt utter terror—a trusted friend was raping me. Flashbacks of the abortion flooded my mind. I cried and cried and demanded that he go get my purse and find my package of birth control pills so that I could take one, and make sure I was not getting pregnant again.

I was beyond horrified. I was paralyzed with fear. Not only over the fact that I'd passed out and was so out of it that I had no idea what was happening to my body—but that I was being raped—and by a friend. But I was *hysterical* that I could possibly get pregnant again. I certainly was not going to have another abortion, and I sure did not want this guy to be the father of my child.

I broke. I told him that I'd had an abortion and could not get pregnant again! I don't remember how he responded, but at least he stopped.

He returned to the bed with my purse and my pills inside, and found me sobbing. He kept repeating, "Shhhh … shhhhhh …" until I passed out again.

I don't remember anything else up until a point later the next day … I was still drunk. We had to check out of the hotel, I guess. I hazily remember walking to a lake somewhere with some of the friends from the party, including the rapist lust-monger, who turned into my nursemaid that day. Apparently no one else at the party knew what he had been doing to me in the other room, and I was still too smashed to even speak.

I don't remember leaving our party post or the drive to whatever lake we visited. I only remember being coherent enough to wake up for a short while as two friends helped me walk over gravel to get to a boat. One of the "crutches" was Raper Guy. I couldn't refuse his helping me to walk—over twelve hours later I'd not regained control over my body. I was still a rag-doll limp-noodle skunk-drunk zombie. Of course I was still not able to walk straight and stumbled on the gravel around the dock.

We climbed into a small gray metal dinghy powered by oars, and the motion of the choppy water and jerked rowing movements sent any remaining stomach acid over the edge of the boat for the duration of the ride. A hangover wasn't the only thing I was dealing with in the rough water. I ached with tremendous pain from the rape and the bumpy ride on the metal seat brought tears down my face as I passed out again. I was so sick that it took three days to recover from the alcohol I had consumed.

My parents were out of town on business and had no idea what was happening back home.

I confronted the rapist weeks later and asked him why on earth he had done it. He smugly and contentedly replied with a grin, "It's just something I always wanted to do."

How creepy is that? I was not a friend to him; I was nothing more than an object of his lust.

If only I would have stayed sober. If only the "supervising" adult had not purchased the alcohol for us. Would Raper still have raped his "friend"?

If only I would have learned how to say no back when I was in grade school—or at any point in my life. But, I didn't know I was in danger ... did not even see it coming.

I wonder how many unintended pregnancies or rapes result at the tail end of an adult's "cool" choice to be the "friend" to buy underage kids alcohol. I wonder how many unintended pregnancies occur because people are inebriated out of their normal reasoning capacity.

My rapist was not some random stranger whom I would never see again. He was my classmate and ran in the same circle of friends that I did. I had to face him every day.

I talked about "Raper Creeper" to a few of my closest friends but don't remember anything about their responses or what was said, only that they were not surprised because of the guy's reputation. My friends were just kids like I was. I don't remember them bringing up the idea to report it to an adult either. I never even thought to report it to the police, like I should have. I was scared that I'd get in trouble for drinking alcohol. It just seemed like "one of those things" that happens when girls get drunk ... don't ever buy that. Rape is never acceptable.

Near prom week, a girlfriend invited a group of us to her house for a swimming party. I was looking forward to kicking back with a bunch of friends and having a good time. I'd have to arrive late because my year-end dance recital was coming up soon, so practices were extended and more intense.

After class ended, I rushed to the girl's house; everyone else was already there—at least twenty-five to thirty people were in or around the pool.

I'd worn my swimsuit under my dancing costume, so I could change all the more quickly and join the party. But the moment I left the diving board and hit the water, I was hit with an intense charley horse in my left thigh. In a hurry to escape the dance studio, I'd not cooled down after dancing hard.

I was in the deep end struggling to keep my head above water as the pain was exacerbated with every movement. I flailed around to find the edge of the pool for safety but couldn't get very far before my head went under again. The desperation for oxygen only worsened the cramp in my leg. The music was too loud for my girlfriends only a few feet away to hear me hollering for a hand to pull me into shallower water. I squeezed my eyes shut as I pounded my thigh with one fist, treading water with my other arm and leg.

I felt the splash of someone dive in beside me and hoist me above water enough to find air. I grabbed on tightly to the arms that secured my space above the splashing and looked square in the face of the guy who had raped me.

"What's going on?" he asked.

I told him about the cramp in my leg. He quickly grabbed it and rubbed out the knot until it was gone.

I was angry that the one who had abused me had possibly saved my life. A rush of emotion overtook me. He asked if I was OK. I shook my head yes, swam away, and found an excuse to leave the party early.

Another night was spent crying myself to sleep.

When we saw each other at school, my hatred toward him began to soften ... he had, after all, rescued me. A seed of forgiveness began to take root in my heart. He could have let me drown. It didn't seem that his prior intent was to hurt me. He just happened to be a first-rate jerk. At the pool party, he'd never made a move on me—probably knowing that especially in front of our other friends I'd have absolutely pitched a west Texas hissy fit. He knew I didn't like him in that way. He had simply wanted to steal what he knew he would never be given. Arrogance does that. It takes what it thinks it deserves, without counting the cost. Love waits.

I cannot begin to understand what it must be like for those who have been raped under vicious circumstances—what I experienced was incomprehensible enough.

As days passed and graduation emotions burned strongly, I thought about leaving all my friends behind—most of whom I would never see again. I thought about that guy, and while I didn't want to ever see him again after I had my diploma in my hand, I chose to forgive him. I partially blamed myself—while he did force himself on me, he had not forced the liquor down my throat. He had intensified its potency, but I chose to pick up the cup and drink it. I don't believe that he would've ever beaten me in a violent rape. Not to diminish what he did by any means, he was just not the violent kind of rapist. He was more the creepy kind that probably wouldn't have gone through with his urges had I been sober. Nevertheless, he had raped me, and I should have reported it to the police.

However, I remain fully persuaded that a baby should not be aborted because of his or her biological father's crime of rape. What's worse—rape or murder? Consider this: if a mother's aborting her baby is acceptable because the child would remind the mother of the rapist, then wouldn't that be the same as saying it would've been reasonable for me to have murdered my rapist because he reminded me of the crime that occurred? Every time I saw him after the rape, I was reminded of what he did to me. I saw him every school day until we graduated, and sometimes on weekends at school functions. Should I have been legally allowed to put him to death—because he reminded me of the rape? Of course not.

While we're on the subject—in case anyone out there is wondering—passed out means *no!* Drunk or drugged means *no!* "No" means *no!* Crying means no. Turning away means no. Pushing means no. "Stop" means no. "Get off" means no.

Do not bully your way into where you are not invited physically, or you are a rapist committing a crime worthy of jail. Period.

CHAPTER 10

The Only Way Out

After all that had happened, I could not shake the shame. I mentally calculated all the medical terminology and tried to make myself think that what I had done— the abortion—was merely a medical procedure to extract a "mass" of a "fetus" or "pregnancy tissue"; but in my heart, I sensed all along that there was so much more to it than that. How could it not have been a human? What else could it have been—a pterodactyl dinosaur? Could it have been an alien from outer space threatening our international security? What would it have done if we had let it live? Would it have ruined acres and acres of our corn fields with crop circles?

It is what it is, whether it's the size of a lima bean or the size of your twenty-pound Thanksgiving turkey. It is completely a human being at every stage and that human is *alive*. I know it now—and instinctively, I knew it then.

First the abortion seemed the only way out of our situation. Then I found myself thinking that suicide seemed the only real way out of my despair from the shame of the unplanned pregnancy, the abortion and the rape. I thought about it a lot and considered every possible option to carry it off. I even made a few private attempts but never told anyone about what was happening in my mind.

I kept thinking of what life would be like for my family if I would kill myself. Who would find my body, and what would it do to his or her emotional state of well-being? I could not bear the thought of leaving a mess of my dead body for anyone to clean up—nor of my family having to plan, pay for, and go through a funeral.

I sought wisdom from the expert school counselor.

It was a week or so before I could get an appointment with Mr. Snodgrass who visited the school to listen to students' issues. I was desperate, discouraged, and disappointed that I couldn't see him right away. I was ready to talk. Brock and I never really talked about the abortion after the fact. We just ignored it like it never happened … as if even we "would not know" about the abortion … as if it weren't spoken about, then it didn't really happen.

There were a couple of close friends that knew about the abortion, but they had no clue how to counsel me, and I didn't even know what to ask or how to phrase what was happening in my mind. I needed a professional.

Finally, when it was my day to pour my heart onto the floor of the counselor's office, I was relieved that I was going to get the guidance I needed to be free of my emotional pain. At last I had found someone to make sense of things for me.

I knew our time was short, so I got right to the point and blurted out what I had done. Mr. Snodgrass nodded. He just looked at me through his thick gold-rimmed, aviator-style eyeglasses. He didn't move another muscle, nor did he offer up even a peep of a noise. He didn't even clear his throat.

Maybe he had not heard me. Perhaps he just needed more information—as if having an abortion was not big enough for a reaction. I most certainly was not expecting a response like I had received from my mom—and certainly not one like I had experienced from Brock's mom—but the guy gave me nothing but a poker face.

Thinking he needed all the details to best help me, I dished it all out. At the end of the meeting, all he said was something like, "I hope you feel better—you will be fine."

That was it. Snodgrass did not ask if I wanted to meet again or how I was feeling or what I was thinking. That was the whole extent of the "counseling session" that I had initiated and so eagerly waited for in hopes of coming away with relief. It would have been more effective if I had taken an Alka-Seltzer. He must have missed the "How to Help Someone with Abortion Recovery 101" section in counseling school. Maybe I should have told him that suicidal thoughts had been hammering my brain and that I had been raped too, but I don't think that would have made much of a difference. Besides, wasn't an abortion itself worth talking about to a client? Had I just been a big waste of his time? Who was that guy? Was he really a "counselor"?

I thought about filing a complaint against him with the principal. I was hurt and felt cheated. Now, someone *else* knew the secret that no one was supposed to know. What was the point? But if I had lodged a complaint against him, I thought it would have further exposed what I was supposed to keep hidden. Besides, what did I know about those things? He was the professional that the school brought in to "talk" with us students about "things." I supposed that my "session" was the way the adult world dealt with issues.

I had thought about talking with the youth pastors but figured they wouldn't have anything to really tell me. I was too overcome with guilt and I did not want anyone else to know.

The friend who took me to my first visit at the clinic for the pregnancy test knew, but she and I never talked about it after that. I guess she felt like she had helped me by taking me there.

I did not know how to ask for help.

I never pursued another counselor to talk to about the abortion—I felt it was a little too late to do anything about it anyway since it was already over.

What would that abortionist doctor have done if I would have gone to him for advice ahead of time? The abortionists gave me that Valium pill to "help" me afterward … that pill was not so hard to swallow. So why was having an abortion so hard to swallow? Why did I feel like I continually wanted to throw up for years afterward? Not from anything physically going on in my body—but emotionally. Was it more Valium that I needed? The baby "problem" was "out of the way," so why couldn't I just get on with my life? If the baby was not a baby after all, but a "pregnancy mass" of tissue, what was the big deal anyway? Was I hallucinating, or was I grieving only the "idea" of what it could have been? No. It was a human *baby*—and I knew it. It didn't magically change into a human at a specific gestational phase. I knew it was human from the very start.

I wondered if Brock ever thought about it again. I wonder if he's thought about it even three times in the last thirty years.

I continued to think of suicide for a long time. But I could not do that to my mom. I knew that if I killed myself, it would "kill" her and the other members of my family, all of whom I loved so much. I couldn't do that to them. I understood what suicide does to families because when I was in seventh grade, a friend of mine killed herself.

Jennifer Golden was a peppy and pretty eighth-grade cheerleader with a beautiful big white smile, hazel eyes, and blond highlights in her bouncy spiral perm. I always looked forward to talking with her in our shared seat on the long bus ride home after school because she seemed so full of life.

She came from a well-to-do family and lived in a magnificent house that was professionally decorated in every room and every hallway. Likewise, she was always dressed adorably, right down to the matching accessories. Her life seemed so—perfect. But as I learned and as I was experiencing in my own life, not everything on the surface is as it actually is underneath.

Jennifer's dramatic suicide by a gunshot to the head and the closed casket funeral left such an indelible mark on my mind. I simply could not leave my family with all that I saw her family and friends deal with after her death. The whole school turned out for her funeral, and I saw people crying over her death who I thought didn't even know her. It affected everyone I knew in the town.

While I resolved not to kill myself by any method, I still could not help but feel dead on the inside. I only wished I could become invisible and it would not matter to anyone ... but somehow I knew I mattered to God. And I want you, reader, to know that you matter to God too.

An old Sunday school song from my childhood rolled around in my mind, overriding the fun eighties songs I enjoyed on the new television channel that played music "all day every day." The song goes like this, "Jesus loves me, this I know. For the Bible tells me so. Little ones to Him belong; when we're weak, He makes us strong. Yes, Jesus loves me, yes, Jesus loves me. Yes, Jesus loves me, the Bible tells me so."

One Saturday morning while cleaning my room to qualify for the weekly excursion to Dillard's, I ran across my old familiar bookmark from Isaiah 40:8, *"The grass withers and the flowers fade, but the word of our God stands forever"* (New Living Translation).

I still did not know what *else* the Bible said, but it meant everything to me that the Word of God would *always* be there. I found tremendous comfort in that verse and thought about it all the time. The "Jesus Loves Me" song played repeatedly in my head like a broken record—but I still felt like an enormous hypocrite.

The drunken rape episode did not deter me from drinking. I kept imbibing—a lot, and frequently. But even when I was drunk, my heart was still haunted by all that I had experienced. Neither drugs nor alcohol are real issue solvers. If only chocolate were! Then I would be the most emotionally healthy person on the block.

Wouldn't life be grand if all my hauntings would have vanished by eating a Taco Bell® Soft Taco Supreme®? I love those. No amount of food or even fiber will cleanse the digestive tract to flush out even the smallest amount of pain in the heart. Not even laxatives. Repeated use of those erodes your plumbing.

I know from experience.

I started binge eating. I could eat a whole brick of Neapolitan ice cream, a bag of Tostitos® corn chips, and a big jar of mild Pace picante sauce—as long as I made myself throw it up afterward. During every meal I would slowly savor each bite and count each chew until there was either nothing left between my teeth or I'd counted to a number high enough to satisfy my warped thinking. Within moments of my fork hitting the edge of the plate, I would dash to my bathroom toilet and stick my finger down my throat so that I would not gain any weight.

I was staying in firm shape with the dance classes, spending my lunch hours at school running up and down the stadium bleachers, and riding my bike twenty miles a day on weekends. I could keep eating and eating and eating because nothing stayed in my stomach. I loved the benefits of being thin. I could wear whatever I wanted and at least I felt great physically—for a while, anyway.

Several friends and I were obsessed with comparing ourselves with other girls. We were not "mean girls." I had just become passionate about being perfect—as if outward perfection could hide the mucky grime that coated my insides.

It wasn't long before my throat started to hurt in the middle of the day, even when I wasn't eating or purging, and I knew it was from all of the vomiting. It was a sharp pain, like the back of my throat had been carved out. I hated to puke, even when I was sick, but I liked being able to eat anything I wanted in any amounts and not gain weight. I did not, however, like what I was trading to stay slim. I was conscious about my breath, and after spending so many years in braces and retainers I had grown fond of protecting my teeth. I was troubled that the stomach acid could be ruining the enamel ... and I knew that once enamel is gone, it's gone. Like losing your virginity or having an abortion, there's no going back; it's final.

I became anemic, and I felt weak and tired all the time. I stopped having my periods. The bulimia diet plan worked until I got into college. With the later nights and work schedule, I was simply fatigued by keeping up appearances, plus the side effects weighed heavily on my mind. Eventually I tapered off the barfing and instantly gained ten pounds.

Even now, years later, I still get tempted to make myself throw up after I eat a big meal, but I'll not give in to those thoughts because I don't want to go backwards. I haven't "tossed my cookies" on purpose since college; and I think that if I were to do it once, it would be hard to stop. I don't want to reopen any old wounds like that and don't want to have to re-break that old disgusting habit. I'm amazed that after thirty years, purging is still a temptation.

The human body is magnificently created to grow scabs to protect open sores and give injuries time to heal. But the lacerations on my soul didn't get much relief from time itself. Just when I felt like I was forgetting about what had happened I'd notice another baby in a store or on television or someone would talk about something that would trigger the memory of what had happened. This caused the thin scab to be pricked from the surface of my heart, and the pus would again flow from my battle sores.

At the tail end of my senior year, my best friend and my new boyfriend, Jeff Sparks, talked to me about Psalm 23 in a way that I'd never heard before. He shared a book with me that expounds upon the Psalm.[7] It is a beautiful portrait likening human nature to the nature of silly sheep that go astray and get into trouble when they wander off on their own. When sheep follow each other in a mob-frenzy way, they get into the craziest tangled-up messes. The book's focus is also about the nature of God as a shepherd who tenderly, patiently, and lovingly looks after His flock to feed them, to guide them, and to protect them from wolves.

One translation of the Bible I like is the *Amplified Bible*. In it, Psalm 23 goes like this:

> *The Lord is my Shepherd [to feed, guide, and shield me], I shall not lack.*
>
> *He makes me lie down in [fresh, tender] green pastures; He leads me beside the still and restful waters.*
>
> *He refreshes and restores my life (my self); He leads me in the paths of righteousness [uprightness and right standing with Him—not for my earning it, but] for His name's sake.*
>
> *Yes, though I walk through the [deep, sunless] valley of the shadow of death, I will fear or dread no evil, for You are with me; Your rod [to protect] and Your staff [to guide], they comfort me.*
>
> *You prepare a table before me in the presence of my enemies. You anoint my head with oil; my [brimming] cup runs over.*
>
> *Surely or only goodness, mercy, and unfailing love shall follow me all the days of my life, and through the length of my days the house of the Lord [and His presence] shall be my dwelling place.*

Jeff shared much with me about God that brought peace and comfort to my soul, so healing started to take shape. Jeff was compassionate and good to me. He was a wonderful and important person in my life, and when he shared the Word of God from the Bible with me, the Holy Spirit would often remind me of the verse that I'd learned as a child.

Although I went to church with Brock, he never talked to me about God or shared anything from the Bible with me. Church just happened to be another place we went. But through Jeff, I began to see God as a *good* shepherd, rather than a harsh judge like how I perceived church people to be; and it made me want to get to know what God is really like.

Because I was getting to know Jesus as the "Rock of my Salvation," I sensed my gyrating emotional free fall beginning to slow down. I began to find a pointed course, and could somewhat sense earth beneath my feet again.

I could see the light at the end of the tunnel; I was just not sure how to get across the great divide that I felt was between me and the end.

CHAPTER 11

The Hardest Thing

G raduation Day came on May 20, 1984, and at six o'clock the following morning I was on a plane bound for Tulsa, Oklahoma, to live with my other set of parents and go to college. I was ready for a change of pace from my old home town—I needed to find a new environment.

Jeff had gone off to a different college, and we drifted apart.

By August I had found a job at the first place I applied … yup, at Dillard's, where else? Shopping at Dillard's was what I knew well! During training I made fast friends with two coworkers, Nadia and Kourtney, who had just graduated and moved to Tulsa to attend college as well, but not the school I was attending—they were going to a Bible school.

Almost every night after Woodland Hills Mall would close and we would get off work at 9:15, a group of us headed to a twenty-four-hour coffee shop to finish homework. The books they were reading piqued my interest far more than those from my journalism classes.

The first book of theirs that I read was written by Kenneth E. Hagin, the founder of the Bible school, and was titled,

What Faith Is. The short read only roused my hunger for more. As I finished the last page and closed the book, I felt like I had taken one bite of Christmas dinner's full table offerings and had to put down the fork without being satisfied. I wanted to dive into everything my spiritual eyes were seeing. I wanted to stay at the table for seconds and thirds, linger in my dining room chair for an hour to let digestion commence, then promptly dig in again up to my elbows. I felt like I had found "home."

The more I heard about what they were learning, the more I sensed I'd pushed God into my back pocket. My light was snuffed out under a bushel full of scandalous cover-up. That light went out back when I believed I *had* to take the life growing within my body so *church* people wouldn't know I'd had premarital sex—especially since it was with the son of a couple involved in church management.

The disgrace I felt was nonstop. All the church people may as well have known! What shame would "the others" have felt if I had kept the baby living and given it up for adoption—or if I had kept him or her to raise on my own? Would their dishonor compare to what I was experiencing? Would I have felt as much shame if I had gone through high school pregnant? Did the congregation members firmly believe their sermons and their lyrics to the hymns?

We so proudly lifted our voices to the cross above the baptismal and stained glass with words like this:

> There is a fountain filled with blood drawn from
> Emmanuel's veins;
> And sinners plunged beneath that flood lose all
> their guilty stains.

Lose all their guilty stains, lose all their guilty
stains;
And sinners plunged beneath that flood lose all
their guilty stains.[8]

Did those words not apply to me and my boyfriend? Or had we insulted God so deeply that our sin could never be forgiven?

I carry a scar on my right wrist as a reminder of "The Suicide That Wasn't." The scar did not come from an object at my own hand in an attempt to take my life.

I had, however, once trembled with my mom's finest cutlery at the pulse point of my wrist. I imagined a TV-drama-like scene as I watched my flesh begin to yield to the blade. In desperation and fear of only landing in the hospital rather than the cemetery (not to mention the fear of leaving my family's souls scarred for life), I put the knife away and slumped into a heap on the floor. I bawled until I had no more tears to release and my cheeks stung from the salty drops, and retreated to my room before anyone came home.

Everything seemed better from under the comforter on my own bed. On the shelf of my headboard I found that old bookmarker with that familiar Bible verse. My sobs weakened as I trusted in those words, *"The grass withers and the flowers fade, but the word of our God stands forever."*

Whatever grass or flowers that had been around me sure had withered and faded; I needed something that could stand forever so I could find footing again and climb out of my darkness. I was beginning to see that God was offering a hand up.

While a reminder of my despair, the scar on my wrist happens to be from a wound sustained during a visit with an old friend, Gabrielle. I had just opened the door to her dorm room and stepped inside when I slipped on the freshly mopped tile floor. Still holding onto the door, the weight of my body threw my arm against the door's hardware and slit my wrist slightly. It narrowly missed a major artery, yet sliced it perfectly to ooze enough blood and leave a slight scar that no one has ever mentioned. Nevertheless it's visible enough to me that it serves as a bookmarker to a long-ago chapter of my life that could have been cut short.

That first year of college was a busy one; I was working full time and taking fifteen hours of classes, but I began to study my coworkers' Bible school books along with my own homework. I wanted to know everything they knew about God and wanted to be around them all the time. They were fun and could have fun—without alcohol.

One typical Oklahoma muggy day, my two new friends from work and I went swimming, and somehow we got on the subject of girl stuff. I confided in them that it had been a year since I'd had my period. What I did not tell them was that it was likely because of my extreme exercise and bulimia.

It made me wonder if I'd ever be able to get pregnant again.

To my surprise, both girls piped up boldly telling me that God wanted me to be healthy and that He could heal my body and make it normal again. I balked at how "silly" it would be to pray and ask God for such a thing as they were suggesting. I was so surprised by their confidence that I agreed to let them pray with me right then—out of sheer curiosity, not because of my own faith. The instant they said "amen," I went into the bathroom and lo and behold *at that moment* my body responded to their faith in our good God who cared that I should have a normal cycle! The evidence was clear. After a solid year of amenorrhea, my body was instantly healed. Was it a fluke? A coincidence? For me, there was no denying that God had just crashed into my world and miraculously showed me His compassion.

The next school year, 1985–86, I dealt with intense migraine headaches that were debilitating. No medication that the doctor prescribed seemed to diminish the pain. The vice grip on my skull would hurl me into my darkened bedroom seeking reprieve. One day at work I mentioned the migraines to a coworker who also happened to be a student at Nadia and Kourtney's Bible school. I told her that the EEG and CT scans were inconclusive and that the prescriptions did not offer any release; the medical community had no answers at that point in my care.

Again, God sent a bold Bible believer to pray for my body and again, He healed me. She sympathetically prayed a quick prayer with me right there amongst the clothing racks on a quiet evening in the mall, and I have *never* had another migraine. Ever. Before, my brain was in extreme anguish and now my mind was totally blown! Who *was* this God who kept amazing me with His goodness? I had to get to know Him better.

By the fall of 1986, I was a full-time student at Rhema Bible Training College learning about the love and nature of God, and I was seeing more of His faithfulness and goodness in my life.

That old familiar verse from Isaiah now meant something much broader to me. I learned about God's unconditional love and unmerited grace, and I saw that God had been with me in spite of my darkest decisions. He was there waiting for me to turn to Him and help pick up the broken pieces of my heart. He loved me enough to let me make my own decisions. Even though His Word clearly tells us that He is not in favor of all the choices we make, He still loves us. His love is not based on what we do or do not do. He loves us simply because that's who He is.

Knowing you have been forgiven of a heinous act is indescribable. Understanding that God could love me no matter what I had done started to make sense the more time I spent getting to know Him. I kept listening intently in Bible school and taking an overabundance of notes ... and I finally allowed myself to receive His unfathomable pardon for my crime. My debt had been paid through the work that Christ did on the cross. How could I not forgive those who had hurt me, when God was forgiving me of so much worse?

The Bible verse John 3:16 made perfect sense to me now— *"For God so loved the world, that he gave his only begotten Son, that whosoever believeth in him should not perish, but have everlasting life"* (King James Version). But oh how the next verse shined the light in to the corners of my heart! *"For God sent not his Son into the world to condemn the world; but that the world through him might be saved"* (King James Version).

I am so grateful that God gave us a Bible to show us how He feels about things like this: *"Now there is no condemnation for those who belong to Christ Jesus. And because you belong to him, the power of the life-giving Spirit has freed you from the power of sin that leads to death."* (Romans 8:1–2 New Living Translation).

My Father in heaven was not condemning me! The only condemnation was from the perceived judgment that may have or may not have come from those in church! We never even asked Brock's parents what they would think—I wonder now what their reaction would have been. Maybe he asked them—I don't know, but I was definitely never involved in any conversations about it and there'd been no way I was going to bring it up.

How would Brock's mom have responded to the news if we'd decided to keep the baby? Would I have been locked away in the bell tower of the church with the bats? Would I have been excommunicated? Would anyone have tried to send me away to live in another country?

Why do we torture our own souls with endless questions and perceptions as if they were facts? Thankfully, God's love surpasses all our foolishness; and at the end of the day, He is still waiting right in front of us with outstretched arms and open hands.

One college morning, sunlight spilled into my bedroom through the window and my alarm clock clicked on the radio. The broadcast was Reverend Kenneth E. Hagin, and he was speaking on forgiveness. As he spoke, a thought came to my mind, "If Almighty God can forgive you, who do you think you are not to forgive you?" As blunt as could be—there it was.

My heart had relished in receiving God's compassion, but I had had no mercy on myself. The hardest thing was releasing the bloody guilt I had carried on my back for so long.

I heard Reverend Hagin say that morning on the radio words that Jesus had said. Although those words were thousands of years removed from when Jesus spoke them, it seemed like Jesus was standing in front of me, looking me in the eye, and speaking directly to me:

> *Come to Me, all you who labor and are heavy laden, and I will give you rest. Take My yoke upon you and learn from Me, for I am gentle and lowly in heart, and you will find rest for*

your souls. For My yoke is easy and My burden is light. (Matthew 11:28–30 New King James Version)

Yokes I understood, because Grandpa Hill had raised teams of mules and horses that had been connected with a "yoke" between them, then together they could pull Grandpa's buggy. I had seen his splendid animals, even Clydesdale horses or mule teams working in unison—and I recalled times when a team did not cooperate! I knew Grandpa never would have been able to get his ornery Shetland ponies to work together in that way. I wanted to take on Jesus's yoke and walk His way beside Him. It had to be easier than what I'd been coming up with on my own.

When Jesus said His "burden" was light, I knew He meant by the example that His "cargo" was light. If I'd get hitched to His wagon, the equipment or people or tools I was to carry along life's road with me would be light. That I could sign up for. I was ready to unload my own heavy, muddy, unstable cart with the wheels falling off, and walk in harmony with Him.

The radio preacher wasn't done. He quoted Mark 11:24–26:

[Jesus said,] *Therefore I say to you, whatever things you ask when you pray, believe that you receive them, and you will have them. And whenever you stand praying, if you have anything against anyone, forgive him, that your Father in heaven may also forgive you your trespasses. But if you do not forgive, neither will your Father in heaven forgive your trespasses.* (New King James Version)

I couldn't bear the thought. I had trespassed big time, and faced a new choice. I'd forgiven the creepy rapist, and even Brock's mom for treating me the way she did, in spite of the fact that my heart still hurts every time I think about the encounter with her. I forgave them.

But … I hated myself.

Choosing to forgive *myself* was a difficult and weighty task, not easily handed off, but another scripture came to my heart that simplified the process. It's from 1 Peter 5:7 New King James Version and says, *"Casting all your care upon Him, for He cares for you."*

Casting fishing lures with a fishing pole was another thing I was good at doing, so I imagined myself hurling my cares into God's lake of forgiveness, then cutting the taut line never to reel it in to my shoreline again.

As I rested there in bed that morning listening to the radio message, I wept as I sensed His caring Father-like love for me. I at last heaved my final cares over on Him—God, the One who was, and is so willing to set aside my sin and welcome me into His strong arms of mercy and renewal.

The weight lifted. My burden was gone.

Hardly a day has passed that I don't think about the fact that I have a child in heaven, but the weight of sin is not there anymore. Jesus Christ has set me free.

CHAPTER 12

Every Day

My first baby would have been born in September of 1983. That means I would have a child who has already blown out the candles on his or her thirtieth birthday cake.

Also in the fall of 1983, my cousin Brad was born. I've watched every milestone of his life as a marker of what my child might have been doing if I had let him or her live. Brad is married and has a baby of his own. Wow … to think that I could be a grandma … and possibly a mother-in-law! What would my grandchildren call me? Grandma Kristan? Or maybe Neni, like my kids call my mom? Would they call me Grandmama like I called my mom's mom or even Memaw like my kids call my mother-in-law?

I married a wonderful man named Scott Gray who is a great and involved father for our three children.

We first met when I answered the door when he came to pick up my roommate for a date.

That's the simple version, anyway—at least that's the first time we talked.

Scott stepped inside, took one look at me, and deep down in the depths of his being, he sensed a strong impression rising up on the inside of him. He heard God speak to his heart, "*That's your wife.*"

Have you ever been driving down the road and had a feeling that you should take a different route home? He described it as being much like that—a knowing inside that I would be his wife.

You can imagine how awkward it was, then, when my tall gorgeous Norwegian roommate, Tammy Klein, stepped into the living room to go out with him. They were not serious boyfriend and girlfriend but were going to hang out together.

I sensed nothing remotely close to what he had that night, and thankfully he didn't scare me off by telling me what was going on inside his head. He was living in Iowa and was visiting Tulsa for an alumni event. He wisely put the idea on a shelf in the back of his mind. Our conversation was a brief casual exchange in the entryway while waiting the few minutes before Tammy was ready.

He left my apartment after our entry-way encounter, went out with my roommate, then went back to his home in southwest Iowa the next day. For two and a half years, he toyed with moving back to Tulsa to explore that idea that had popped into his head at my door. Was it was for real? Had he truly heard from God as he believed? Or, was it the spicy food he had eaten the night before that had spoken to him?

When he conceded, he threw a Hail-Mary prayer pass, "OK, God. I'll move back to Tulsa and trust that You will get me a great job, show me where to go to church, set me up with a good apartment and roommate, and I will do it," he vowed. "I'll move there and see what happens. If Kristan is still living there, still single, and would be interested in going out with me, then so be it. If not, I'll leave that with You."

That was May of 1989. The apartment-door encounter had taken place in October of 1986. Scott didn't even know whether or not I still lived in Tulsa, but acting on faith that it was God who was leading him, he concentrated on getting settled before he began his search for me. He still had friends there, so if the whole idea turned out amiss, at least Tulsa, Oklahoma, wasn't the end of the line for him.

Eventually, in November of that year—over three years after we'd met—we ran into each other. All those months he'd been living in Tulsa again, he'd been serving as an usher at the same church where I was a youth leader. But the youth met in a separate area, so our paths never crossed until the youth joined the adults one Wednesday night for a special event. I sat in front of Scott, not even realizing he was sitting there.

He was quick to tap me on the shoulder; I was quick to light up when I recognized him. We chatted for a while; I blushed through the whole service. It had been a sparky encounter. For the next hour during church, he squirmed in his seat, monitoring the time on his watch as he rallied the courage to ask me out.

At the conclusion of the service, I slowly turned around to see if he was still there or if he'd cut out the back door. He was there all right, shifting his feet from right to left and back again, trying to look cool, but he clearly liked talking to me. I blushed again. He leaned in and asked, "Would you like to go out for coffee next Wednesday night after church?"

How could I say no? He was cute and had a firm handshake that sealed the deal. I was as excited as I'd been as a little girl the first time my dad took me to the new Baskin Robbins ice cream store that had thirty-one flavors! There were several guys I was spending time with—not thirty-one of them—but some; none of them steadily. He was like the German-chocolate ice-cream flavor. I was not going to settle for Rocky Road or Baseball Nut again.

Two days before we were to go out for dinner, I answered the phone at work. It was Scott. He seemed surprised that I was on the other end.

"Hmm. That's weird," I thought. "Why would he call me and then be surprised that I am here?"

As we talked, he informed me that he was actually calling to talk to my co-worker, his roommate! Another coincidence? Or had God set it up? Here we had been attending the same church for months and had never known it. He had had no idea that his roommate worked with me. He'd never told anyone about his experience at my door, so his roommate never would have thought to tell him, "Oh, by the way, I work with her!"

Our first date, after church—Wednesday, November 15, 1989—he strolled over to the youth area to get me. We went to a restaurant and found conversation banter was delightfully engaging and fun.

Midstream in getting to know each other, a policeman with a rifle in his hands burst through the front door shouting, "Everyone get under the tables!"

He rushed to where we were sitting and yelled, "Get away from the windows! There's a man outside by the hotel—shooting!"

We raced to the center of the room and dove for cover. We didn't hear any shots being fired—only shouting coming from the throng of police outside. There'd been a domestic dispute in the parking lot, but the situation was averted. It was an interesting bonding experience, to say the least!

Scott told me, "I'll take you back to your car at the church and follow you home to make sure you get there safely—hopefully there are no more madmen out tonight!"

I knew he'd partially been joking but was glad he seemed to be a good caretaker.

When he pulled into the parking spot next to my car in front of my apartment, he jumped out and hammered, "*This* is where you live?"

I'd moved into a different apartment after graduation. Surprisingly, he was living in the same apartment complex as mine! Here Scott was right in the middle of my world—church, work, *and* apartment complex—in a city area of about half a million people. Some might call it fate, others might say serendipity or a fluke, but I like to think it was indeed God who led us to each other, and we made the choice to go along with it.

By New Year's Eve I knew I wanted to marry him.

That January birthday came around and for my twenty-fourth, he created a week-long celebration for me. Every night or day we did something fun or went somewhere amazing, like to a Broadway play—and ate dinner *sitting on chairs* at a restaurant. Scott made my celebration a bigger birthday-palooza than my family ever had! I was convinced that he truly loved me—for me.

What a world away my twenty-fourth birthday was from my seventeenth.

He didn't wait long to propose; we married May 27, 1990.

Thankfully, Scott didn't tell me about what he felt God put on his heart about my being his wife until after he put a ring on my finger.

I waited until after we were engaged to tell him about my abortion. He graciously let me know that he loved me in spite of my past.

The day I said "I do" with a real minister (not a sixth-grade classmate), I was twenty-four and he turned twenty-five during our honeymoon. The man I longed for had come all the way from the Morningside of the Mountain. As it turns out, that mountain, for me, was in the Loess Hills of western Iowa.

We were married for three years before I got pregnant with his baby, because I'd decided I didn't want to have kids. I thought it would be too painful emotionally. After all, when I get to heaven and meet my first child face-to-face, how will I explain that there are more children—whom I chose to let live? How will I ever introduce this human being that lived inside me for a few short weeks to siblings? What will I say? I still wrestle with those thoughts but am so grateful that we have kids. I loved every pregnancy with them—I basked in rubbing my swelling stomach and caressed every roll that I felt coming from the lives that grew inside the *safe* harbor of my body.

The day I heard my firstborn's heartbeat in the doctor's office was the *greatest day of my life*. It was a most amazing experience to hear the heartbeat coming through the special device held near my navel. I wanted to stay there all day connecting with that baby I so eagerly looked forward to meeting face-to-face. I was so disappointed when the nurse took the device away and the sound was gone. I asked her if I could lie there awhile and listen to my baby.

She saw the tear fall from my left eye and run down my cheek near her, and she smiled. "Of course you can," she said sweetly and reconnected me with the life … that sound of *life* … coming from *my* womb.

That precious heartbeat resounded in my ears for days after I left the doctor's office, and I remembered a Bible school teacher saying, "God's heartbeat sounds like this, 'PEOple—PEOple—PEOple—PEOple—PEOple—.'"

When my tummy reached the "public property stage" and other women would bend over, caress my stretched-out stomach with their hands, and talk to my baby with their noses to my navel, it was surreal. I finally had a baby that was more than a "bean" or a "mass," and I welcomed their affection for what lay peacefully inside my big bump.

Although I only gained twenty-seven pounds with my first full pregnancy, there's no way I could ever have kept it a secret like I'd considered in high school; there was clearly a baby under my clothes!

If you're pregnant and feel you have to hide it … I pray that you find a point where you can be bold about your choice to allow *life* to continue living inside your amazingly created body. God is working a miracle right behind your belly button! Whatever your situation is, if you're pregnant—you are actively a part of something remarkable and I pray that you find peace and comfort from God. He loves you. You can trust Him to make your life turn out right.

The day I finally was able to hold my firstborn in my hands was only equaled by the day I first held his little brother and then their sister. Babies indeed are gifts straight from heaven.

That's one reason the devil loves snubbing out babies' lives. Satan's hand has been stirring the pot to slaughter infants from the time of the birth of Moses when Satan deceived Pharaoh to kill baby boys born to the Hebrews—to the time of the birth of Jesus Christ when King Herod issued a decree to put to death all of the male infants from two years old and under.

(See Exodus 1:15–22 and Matthew 2:1–16.) Satan had another landslide victory with that renowned U.S. Supreme Court decision in 1973—Roe v. Wade—which granted legal freedom for abortion in the United States.

It's been over thirty years since I had the abortion and eleven thousand days that I have lived with regret over my decision. When I get to heaven, my child there is the first one I want to meet, so I can ask for forgiveness.

I continue to pray that abortions will stop, but I know they never will. But just maybe—one can be prevented by my finally telling my story.

As it turns out, in 1983, alone, my baby was one of 1,575,000 American abortions reported by the Alan Guttmacher Institute of Statistics[9] (an arm of Planned Parenthood) and one of 1,268,987 reported by the Centers for Disease Control.[10] I don't know the reason for the large discrepancy between the two organizations, but using the Guttmacher statistic from that year, that's a population the size of Philadelphia or Phoenix and *double* the population of the city of Detroit. It breaks down to 4,315 babies aborted *every day* that year. According to the most recent census, I now live in a town of 5,169. Imagine the population of a small town being wiped out *every day* in the United States. Or to put it another way, if those abortions were performed around the clock every day of the week that year, that would mean *three babies per second* being extracted from their mother's wombs.

The Guttmacher Institute Web site quotes reports from 1998, 2000, and 2008, which state, "At current rates, at least half of American women will experience an unintended pregnancy by age 45, and, at current rates, one in 10 women will have an abortion by age 20, one in four by age 30." [11] [12] In a more recent Youtube.com video, which was uploaded in 2011, the Guttmacher Institute reports that one in three women will have an abortion by the time they are age 45.[13] In light of this information, imagine that one in three women you know will have—or have had—an abortion. I wonder how many of those have felt the shame that I did and how many of them are truly free emotionally today.

CHAPTER 13

That Momentum Train— Why Abstinence?

So why is sex before marriage considered sin in the eyes of God when He's the One who invented sex in the first place? I had no idea, so I set out to gain more insight into what He may have had in mind.

First of all, we know from the Bible that God is all about *relationship*. The Bible reveals an amazing thread woven throughout every book from the beginning to the end. It's called the "blood covenant." Here's the deal: From cover to cover, God outlined "covenant." That term has lost its much of its meaning in our world today, but it's potent.

In the beginning, God told Adam to "take dominion" of the Garden of Eden because there was an enemy determined to trash it. We know how that turned out. Adam and Eve realized their sin changed their environment and their standing with God, so they made clothes out of fig leaves to cover their sin and shame. For the first time in their lives, they felt embarrassed so they proceeded to create the first manmade religion: "Don't worry, God. I've got this 'covered' with my 'fig-leaf-ism.'"

I did the same thing. I tried to cover up my sin with something ridiculous so no one could know. Then, I'd buried myself beneath masks of pretending to be someone else—anyone other than who I really was.

But pain has a way of oozing into every crack we try to otherwise fill with activities or over-talkativeness, alcohol abuse, over-eating, drugs, or even sex—anything, everything to hide the shame. Left untreated, pain can turn into emotional gangrene, cutting off pieces of our souls, leaving bitterness, anger, resentment, depression, suicidal tendencies, or the desire to lash out and hurt others.

God saw my face behind the masks—and so did my mom. God sees right through to our hearts and is there waiting to better our circumstances, if we'll only ask Him. He promised to *never* leave us or forsake us! (See Hebrews 13:5 New King James Version, emphasis added.)

The Bible says, *"For I am convinced that neither death nor life, neither angels nor demons, neither the present nor the future, nor any powers, neither height nor depth, nor anything else in all creation, will be able to separate us from the love of God that is in Christ Jesus our Lord."* (Romans 8:38–39, New International Version). God showed His great love for us by sending Christ to die for us while we were still sinners! (See Romans 5:8.)

God knew that Adam and Eve's fig-leaf clothes, albeit stylish I'm sure, were no comparison to what they really needed, so *He* initiated a restored *relationship* by seeking *them* out; they'd been trying to hide from Him. He's also endeavoring to deepen

His relationship with each of us, even while we're trying to hide from him.

The Bible says, *"The life of the flesh is in the blood."* (Leviticus 17:11 King James Version). God slew the first animal to provide the life-giving blood necessary to create a cover for their sin. God then made new clothes for them out of the animal skins.

Isn't it interesting that when we happen upon a vehicular accident, the way we determine if the victim is dead or alive is to check for a pulse? A pulse indicates that *blood* is flowing through the person's body ... it's the sign of life.

How are animals cloned? *By blood.* Scientists know that if they're going to create more life—it has to come from a life source. "The life of the flesh is in the blood," just like the Bible tells us.

Blood sacrifice *covered* Adam and Eve's sin. God saw to it that *life* covered death and reunited mankind to God.

Fast forward to Jesus coming into our world. He didn't merely *cover* our sin, but He *washed it away* altogether with *His* blood that He shed on the cross. (See Revelation 1:5.) That is why it was vital for Jesus to lay down His life for us on the cross—once and for all.

Did you ever make a blood-promise pact with a childhood friend? Many of us ceremoniously cut a finger with a Swiss Army pocket knife with our best friend; we intermingled the blood with a secret handshake to seal the deal of our being "friends forever." That is a blood covenant.

Many third-world tribes practice the blood-covenant ritual to symbolize becoming one in every part of life: "What's mine is yours and what's yours is mine. That includes my army, my protection, my provision, my wealth. I take your debt and share the payoff; your enemies are my enemies—we are *together* in *everything we do*."

Thus the marriage blood covenant—God said when the two are joined together they become one flesh. Something spiritual takes place. A man's body was skillfully crafted by God to fit perfectly with a woman's body. At the initial joining of a man with a virgin, an amazing blood covenant occurs for them when the hymen membrane is broken and blood is present from the woman's body. There's no medical purpose for this to happen. It was designed by God who created our bodies as a sign of a life-giving covenant between husband and wife. The word *covenant* is supposed to mean something: it's a promise, a vow, a contract.

When people operate their lives by reading and following God's owner's manual, the Bible, everything performs like a well-oiled machine. When we go back to making our own fig-leaf lives, we get into hot water and lose that place of dominion and joy in life. According to the Bible, we don't get through the pearly gates with a ticket punched full by our own "good" deeds. Jesus paid for our freedom when He donated His life-giving blood *"once and for all"* (Hebrews 10:10 King James Version). He was raised from the dead to new life and anyone who believes in Him will not perish but have everlasting life. (See John 3:16.)

So, abstinence is a nice theory and everything, but how do people in today's culture *not* have sex when living together before marriage is so widely accepted and even teenagers are allowed to have sleepovers with members of the opposite sex? Our eyes are desensitized by the media's sex and flesh frenzy, and fashion designers are sexualizing even our youngest girls.

The topic in so many television shows is about "hooking up" with someone. A person cannot watch one evening of prime-time television without being exposed to premarital sex and women being objectified.

Even many young girls today may say that if someone does not want to have sex, they "just have oral sex"—but the act of sex, by the way, involves any "private part" of the body that would otherwise be covered by a swimsuit. Oral sex is sex. Oral what? Oh, oral *sex*.

So how do you "just say no"? My cousin Lindsey Griffith granted me permission to use her "How to Say No" list with you. The list is in the appendix at the end of this book.

While it's good to have such a list up your sleeve, there are other practical ways to save sex for marriage.

First of all, what is real love? How does the Bible define it?

> *Love is patient and kind. Love knows neither envy nor jealousy. Love is not forward and self-assertive, nor boastful and conceited. She does not behave unbecomingly, nor seek to aggrandize herself, nor blaze out in passionate anger, nor brood over wrongs. She finds no pleasure in injustice done to others, but joyfully sides with the truth. She knows how to be silent; she is full of trust, full of hope, full of patient endurance. Love never fails.* (1 Corinthians 13:4–8 New Testament in Modern Speech)

Troy Hillman of The Truth Ministries posted a blog about these verses that I find interesting:

When we examine pre-marital sex with this passage (1 Corinthians 13) in mind, we can determine the following: it [pre-marital sex] is not patient, it does dishonor others, it is self-seeking, it does delight in evil, and it damages trust. True love must wait for marriage, which sex was designed for. I have also heard it said, "We are going to get married soon, so why not?" There is an issue with this kind of thinking. If you give into temptation now, before marriage, what's to stop you from giving in to temptation (adultery, for example) during marriage?[14]

True love does wait until the wedding night. Love does not push another person to do something he or she does not want to do. Real love will help the boyfriend and girlfriend save themselves for their wedding night, so their marriage bed will be pure. When we love someone, we set them up for success by setting healthy boundaries.

One woman I know told me that when she and her husband were dating, they were together for quite some time and he never even tried to kiss her. She wondered if he really liked her, so one day she finally "made a move" only to have him say, "I'm saving kisses for my wife." Now that's impressive protection of both their purity and of their future marriage. It was also a great way to show his date he respected her and he respected marriage. Furthermore, he knew where he wanted to establish his boundaries.

I sure wish I'd established some sort of line in the sand before I started dating Brock. If I had set the brakes on a sexual relationship before it got rolling, like I'd done with "the Octopus," then a book about my life would read much differently today.

If you feel it's already too late for you, *it's not.* God's grace is here right now to help you, and He will love you through to the end. Abstinence spares countless sexually transmitted diseases, prevents abortion, keeps people from feeling used and wanted "only for one thing," and keeps relationships wholesome as God intends them to be. Abstinence in a relationship also builds trust for fidelity after the wedding vows.

The amazing thing about God's grace is that *it's free.* Living in a God-centered relationship provides the ability to not have to deal with issues of jealousy, because you know you can trust the other person. And, you behave in a way that the one you love can also trust you; true love doesn't "boil over with jealousy." (See 1 Corinthians 13:4 Amplified Bible.)

The Bible has much to say about not participating in sex outside of marriage, but God does not put the ability to have intimate feelings inside of us without providing tools to control those feelings until we are in a proper married relationship. God tells us our bodies are temples of the Holy Spirit. The Holy Spirit will guide you in the way you should go—even when your stomach is contending for that second helping of food or that entire half-gallon of Neapolitan ice cream. The Bible is loaded with practical tools to guide us. We don't have to wander through this world without being surefooted in what we were created to do. *"Guard your heart above all else, for it determines the course of your life"* (Proverbs 4:23 New Living Translation). He promised that if we do these things, we will surely have great success.

Following God's plan for intimacy by keeping sex sacred and preserved only for marriage makes every relationship healthier. When we hop from bed to bed, it's not merely our bodies that are at risk for sexually transmitted diseases; our emotions are affected because we leave a little piece of our hearts there on the sheets with every encounter.

Women and young girls serve themselves well when they keep their bodies modestly covered and sexually pure for only future spouses. Gals need to know that guys have enough of a challenge keeping their minds clean without seductive or immodest attire tempting them. Now I'm *not* saying that sexy clothing *makes* a guy rape a girl; it most assuredly is not the cause. Guys choose what to do with their bodies just like we girls do; nevertheless, I think girls need to be aware that how we dress sends a message. What message do we want to express? God made men to be stimulated by what they see, much more so than women. It would be wise to remember that; that's not something to which all women can relate.

And guys—a girl who works at keeping herself pure for you to sweep her off her feet and live happily ever after with most certainly deserves a man who has saved his eyes, thoughts, and body for only her. Likewise, modest behavior should continue after the wedding vows to help prevent infidelity. That includes guarding our eyes from pornography. Pornography is a trap of Satan and easily leads to addiction!

This amazing thing called sex that God invented is powerful. When practiced improperly, however, even presidents and ministers are not immune to sex scandals, and the abuse of sex impacts nations. This is certainly the case with diminishing life-expectancy rates due to AIDS in Africa. This dreadful disease has knocked out most of the working age segment of society, which in turn impacts industry and the economy, and creates millions of orphans. Africa's life expectancy rate is less than half of America's because of that disease.

Sex is sacred. When it's kept that way, the sex life is gloriously filled with freedom and joy—not fear of hurt, rejection, and disease.

CHAPTER 14

I'm Not Alone

o you remember that section from your high school biology class where the big thick textbook pointed out the human anatomy reproductive parts? When I was in high school, there was only one small segment of a Chapter that discussed it, but in 2011, when my firstborn son was a junior in high school, he received a supremely different biology lesson than I had.

Near the end of the school year, track season was starting, trees were beginning to bloom again and signs of life were filling our landscape. It had been a long winter and I was glad for the warmth of a spring day. On my way to lunch that fresh Friday afternoon, I grabbed my cell phone and texted my husband and oldest son to see if they'd like to join me for my favorite food—chips and salsa and a little Mexican anything else on the side.

As the tortilla chip basket emptied, our son asked if he could skip school for the rest of the day. His next class "just" had a guest speaker who'd been there all week, and he only had one more class after the guest's lecture. He'd never made such a request and it took me by surprise that he'd even ask. I considered his grades and good behavior and recalled my parents rewarding me for hard work when I had been an upperclassman. Scott and I agreed that he could come home for a break before he went to work. We'd never let him skip a class before, so Scott and I were surprised that we both agreed to let him do it.

On Scott's way home, he stopped at the post office. As he walked back to his car, another parent from our school was driving by, saw Scott, and came to a stop in the road beside him.

"What do you think about the guest speaker at school?" she asked. She also inquired if he knew what they had been talking about in that class. He had no idea.

We learned that in the class our son wanted to skip, the students were in their last day of a two-week lecture that was, in essence, sexology—not biology. Parents had never been informed that their young pliable teens were not only being taught anatomy, but they were being given lessons on the how-tos of sex.

Reports from students varied, but many reported that they were told by the visiting speaker that if anyone became pregnant unexpectedly, it could be "taken care of" with an abortion—no problem. It was as if a pregnant girl would be handed a big pink eraser from a kindergarten school supply box—pregnancy could be erased effortlessly. Humph. "No problem"?

I don't have a problem, per se, with sex education. My issue was more the light manner in which abortion was allegedly presented.

Thankfully, a swift-acting principal altered the course for students the following years. The principal enforced that students thereafter receive a much tamer lesson and parents were given a heads up.

News traveled fast in our small community, and soon parents all over town were in the know about what had happened. At the next school board meeting, parents were exceptionally vocal about the issue. That's where, for the first time since I had had my abortion, I talked in depth with someone else who had experienced one. I was not alone.

Meet Janice. She had an abortion when she was twenty-one years old. She was still working through its aftereffects over thirty years later, and she bravely stood up in the school board meeting and told the room full of people her story of that life-changing incident. She went public. Janice went on to plead with them to change such a format for our students the following school year.

Kids these days already know *how* to have sex and that abortion is an option—but do they know about abortion's aftereffects? Why aren't the students taught about that?

In 1980, when Janice went home for her grandmother's funeral, she was pregnant but did not know it yet. She would soon deal with compounded grief.

She had been working the front desk at a Holiday Inn Hotel that also had a restaurant. She worked a three o'clock p.m. to eleven o'clock p.m. shift and saw many regular customers come past her desk and go into the restaurant for their evening meal or late coffee. One such customer was a deputy sheriff who would regularly come in at night during his supper break.

Janice and Deputy Drake struck up a friendly relationship rather quickly. She was young and tall, pretty, with high cheek bones and deep blue eyes. He knew well how to carry himself in a uniform. The deputy would often swagger up to the desk where she would be assisting hotel patrons and strike up a conversation with her, but their casual chats grew more serious the more time they spent together. Janice made it clear that she was not dating anyone, and he was open about his failing marriage, saying he was "just a signature away from being divorced."

Drake began dropping by her apartment after they both got off work. They felt so comfortable talking with each other and a friendship was easy. Eventually his short visits began to lengthen and the "getting-to-know-yous" lingered. It wasn't long before Janice found herself falling in love with this strong presence in her life, and on a number of occasions Drake told her he loved her and that he wanted to marry her. That's when their relationship turned physical and it wasn't long before Janice realized she was late for her period. She didn't think much of it, but after several weeks without any sign of one on the way, she began to notice other changes in her body, that indicated a possible pregnancy. She bought a pregnancy test from a local store; her results indicated that yes, she was pregnant.

Janice didn't believe it and quickly rushed to the store and bought another test for a second opinion. To be fully persuaded, she bought another one a couple of days later. After three tests, she could no longer ignore the high probability that she was pregnant. Still, she decided to go to a clinic for a professional test, which also proved she was most certainly just as pregnant by the fourth test as she had been with the first one.

By this time Janice was madly in love with Drake and dreamed of spending the rest of her life with him and their baby. She started daydreaming of how soon they would marry and continue to grow their family. But the realization that she was single and pregnant by a man whose divorce wasn't yet final overwhelmed her, and she did not know how to tell him that she was pregnant. Her rapidly changing body, however, forced her to make the decision to inform him.

After mustering up the courage one night, she called Drake at the sheriff's office to arrange a time when he could come over for dinner to give him the news. The dispatcher on call told her that he wasn't there but he was at the hospital.

Janice knew the dangers of men who carry guns and chase bad guys for a living and was worried about what had happened. Why had he been hospitalized? Had he been shot? Had he been in a rollover car accident after a high-speed chase? What could be the reason?

Sensing her concern, the voice on the other end of the phone told her, "Drake is fine! His wife just had a baby!"

Drake had told Janice that he was still living in the house with his wife but had been living in the basement—and that they had *not* been together! He had said he was only staying there until the divorce was final!

The life Janice had dreamed of was instantly shattered. She felt that the love she had received from her law enforcement officer should be trustworthy! It couldn't be true! She found out what hospital they were in and immediately called and asked for their room.

Drake picked up the phone.

Janice frankly blurted out, "I understand that your wife had a baby."

"Yeah," was all he said—she knew he recognized her voice and there was a long awkward silence.

Janice slapped him with, "Well congratulations, you son of a b– because I'm pregnant too," and hung up the phone.

Several nights passed and Janice was numb from the shock of rejection, lies, and pain. She was quite surprised when she looked up one night at work to see Drake standing in front of her at the desk. He looked her square in the face and told her he did not want any part of the baby's life and that their relationship was over. He then turned around and walked out of her life.

Devastating realization smacked hard and deep into her mind … she was in this alone. She didn't know what to do. She felt strongly that she could not go to her family or tell anyone about her dilemma, and she didn't have any extra money to find solutions. She was barely getting by on her small service-industry salary. It was just enough to keep the lights on in her small efficiency apartment.

Not many nights later, she was at work still reeling with confusion when a wonderfully kind and handsome man, not much older than she, approached the hotel desk to check in to the hotel. She and David Hathaway struck up a conversation, chatting lightly before he retired to his room to drop off his bags.

A little later, he came down to have dinner in the restaurant with his business associate, a man with a fatherly air about him. On Janice's dinner break, she went into the restaurant to find the two still sitting at the table. They asked her to join them, so she happily sat down, glad that she wouldn't have to eat dinner alone again.

David and Janice easily picked up their conversation from earlier. The older gentleman seemed to gently nudge the two of them toward each other, which as it turned out, was unnecessary, as she was already drawn to David's personality and his kind ways—and he was clearly attracted to her.

Janice's break was soon over, and she went back to finish her shift. When David had finished eating, he lingered at her desk. He let her know he was not attached to anyone and he treated her respectfully. She savored what seemed to be a genuine interest in her. Not wanting his attention to end, she invited him back to her place after her shift ended. She dreaded the idea of going home to an empty apartment where she would be alone with her thoughts.

The fluid conversation continued at the apartment just as easily as it had at the hotel; however, at some point the mood shifted and things turned romantic. Before she knew it, they had slept together. After a while he went back to the hotel.

When Janice went to work the next day, David had already checked out of the hotel and returned to his home in another state.

A few days later, the thought struck her that he could be the answer to her pregnancy problem, so she looked up his phone number in the hotel records and after a couple of weeks she contacted him and told him she was pregnant.

He was surprised because they had only slept together the one time. He reiterated that he liked her but stated that he did not want a child at that time. Being the nice man that he was, however, he drove back to her city and took her to a clinic and paid for her to abort the baby, all without knowing that the baby was not actually his. Naturally Janice had conflicting feelings about the plan she had set into motion, but she felt there was no other way out.

She thought she would be the only one in the clinic and that the people working there would all be looking at her judgingly. But she was amazed at how many other women were there; the room was full! She wondered if all the others were as terrified as she was of what was about to happen.

When they called her name, they took her into a room to visit with a counselor who explained what was going to happen and what the alternatives were. If she were to go through with the pregnancy, there was no way to hide it. To further compound the issue, how could she explain that not only was she pregnant with a married man's baby, but the man was quite prominent in their community?

"Are you sure of your decision?" the counselor asked.

Janice was anything but sure. By this time, she was nearly three months pregnant and had seen the advertisements showing pictures of babies in the womb. On the day she stepped into that building, she knew where the baby was in the developmental stage. Even still, she made the tough decision to "take care of it" by way of abortion.

Janice vividly recalls the painful feeling of the cervix being forced open and the loud sound of the machine. She lay still through the pain telling herself she deserved every bit of the agony. She even wished that it would have been more painful because of what she was doing, not only to the growing baby inside of her, but to David who was waiting in the other room.

As she rested in the recovery area, she heard another young woman say, "Oh, it didn't hurt me at all." Janice couldn't believe it.

Janice received instructions to take it easy, watch for bleeding, and report any odd symptoms. David drove her back to her apartment and dropped her off. As tears rolled down her face, another man walked out of her life forever. She cried for the rest of the day.

She didn't expect to ever hear from David after he drove away from her apartment. She didn't want to talk to him because it would only remind her she had used him to pay for the abortion of a baby that he'd been cheated into thinking was his. To this day, she has lived with double regret and says the second act of deceiving the nice man has been almost as bad as having the abortion.

Desperate people do desperate things.

A few days later, Janice answered the phone at work and heard a strange woman's voice on the other end of the line demanding, "Is this Janice? Are you pregnant with the cop's kid? 'Cuz I heard that you were."

Janice had no idea what to say but belted out, "Well I don't know where you got your information because it's wrong—I'm not pregnant!" She wasn't lying. She wasn't pregnant—anymore.

"Well, I was just wondering," slowed the voice on the other end, "... because I'm pregnant by him too."

Shell shocked, Janice wouldn't admit she had been pregnant and said, "Well nope, I'm not."

That was that.

Janice knew Drake had to have been the one to tell the woman about her being pregnant, because she had told no one. But why would he tell this other woman? She'd never know.

Because of what she had gone through, Janice developed an eating disorder. Food became her weapon of choice. For the next four years after the abortion, she would starve herself for days then binge eat and follow up with laxatives. Then she would gain weight because she felt she didn't deserve to be happy and she was always happier when her weight was down. She got caught in a vicious cycle of gaining up to fifty pounds or more only to go on crash diets to lose it again.

During one yo-yo phase, she met a man who was in a top-forties band and was asked to join his group as a lead singer. Mr. Guitar Man didn't help her self-image issues, though, because he had subscriptions to several adult magazines filled with women's bodies in air-brush-perfect shape. At the same time, he wanted Janice to eat all the time, even at two o'clock in the morning when they had finished performing a show. The two were engaged for a season and at one point while with him, Janice tipped the scale at 205 pounds from all the late-night and constant eating. She finally broke up with the man, moved back to her home town for six months to get on her feet financially, and lose the weight again.

Between 1984 and 1985 her eating disorder and laxative consumption became dramatically out of control. One Sunday afternoon Janice's stomach was in so much pain that she could not stand up straight. She called her sister to take her to the hospital and the doctors quickly diagnosed her with bulimarexia, a combination of bulimia and anorexia. The specialists insisted that she stay in the hospital until the following weekend, so she could receive properly monitored care and a daily visit from a nutritionist. She needed to get on some kind of a regular healthy eating schedule. It worked for a while, as long as she continued to see the nutritionist.

Shortly after she was released from the hospital, she moved into an apartment with her younger sister. Settling into her new life involved settling some old issues. She knew she had to tell her parents what was really going on in her life ... especially about the abortion. More importantly, she had to know if they could forgive her. She didn't know what she would do to herself if they would not forgive her. Janice said she would not have committed suicide, yet her abuse of food and low body weight had landed her in the hospital.

She called her mom and dad and said, "I need to talk to you and it's serious." They drove down the next day and Janice told them why she had been punishing herself with food. She confided in them everything she was truly thinking and feeling … that she would tell herself she didn't deserve to feel good about herself so she'd purposefully gain weight. She told them about the hospitalization—and the abortion.

Her mom didn't say much at first and she doesn't even remember if her dad had remained quiet before he made a touching statement. Sitting next to her on the couch, his loving response to her news was to simply quote a Bible verse, "As far as the east is from the west is how far God has removed your transgressions from you." (See Psalm 103:12.)

Janice was so overwhelmed by his response of love and tender compassion that she couldn't speak. His words echoed in her heart, and it was in that silence that her mother spoke up, "I don't know if I would have been able to deal with this several years ago, but we have been through some other things since then." With that, Janice was forgiven by the people who loved her most. She, however, she still struggled to forgive herself.

Three years later and a year and a half into a marriage, she gave birth to a son. She had accepted Christ as her Savior when she was young, but it was at the birth of her child that her relationship with Jesus started to become more real to her.

Her mom stayed with her for a while to help with the baby. One day at breakfast, Janice confided in her, "I was really afraid that I would never be able to get pregnant again. God gave me another chance." It was then that she was able to begin to forgive herself.

Several years later, God blessed her with a beautiful daughter.

Still, thirty years removed, she is dealing with the effects of her past. If she eats the wrong thing it causes horrible pain in her stomach because of irritable bowel syndrome created by the laxative abuse. It seems there are constant reminders.

A billboard stands within view of her kitchen window. One season it was plastered with a precious smiling baby crawling on a white rug and a slogan that read, "Choose life. Call for crisis pregnancy help...." Every morning she drove to work, she saw the billboard that served as a daily reminder of what she had done. On one particular morning, however, she noticed the shadow of a cross on the side of the baby's face. The sun was casting a shadow in the shape of the cross from a telephone pole. It was as though God was speaking to her heart, making His own billboard just for her saying, "You're forgiven." She has forgiven herself as well, and for the past several years she has grown tremendously by spending time reading the Bible and fellowshipping with God.

Janice echoes my experience: Abortion clinics tell young women that they can "take care of it" if they get pregnant and it will all go away and it will all be fine—but it's not. It's an acutely traumatic experience spiritually, physically, mentally, and emotionally.

Janice said, "Ya know ... there are some things that you just can't forget."

CHAPTER 15

Babies Are Human Too

I feel passionate that we need to legally *humanize* unborn babies.

In May of 1923, Hitler declared in a speech, "The Jews are undoubtedly a race, but not human. They cannot be human in the sense of being an image of God, the Eternal."

He gained enormous support of others by dehumanizing an entire race of people. It's difficult to fathom today, but people bought his wicked deception! As a result, an estimated six million Jews were brutally and inexcusably murdered.

What is the difference between dehumanizing Jews and dehumanizing babies in order to exterminate them? Does merely changing the status from "being human" justify the means of killing people? Is a baby a human? Is a fetus a human? Emphatically *yes!*

My connection with abortion and the Holocaust was made when I saw the thirty-three minute movie called *180 Movie* on this subject by Way of the Master ministries.[15]

A fetus *is* a *human*. Yet the National Abortion Federation *boasts* 1.3 million abortions occur yearly—every year 1.3

million *humans* are put to death while their mothers defend *their* own rights.[16]

Greg Koukl said, "If the unborn is not a human person, no justification for abortion is necessary. However, if the unborn is a human person, no justification for abortion is adequate."[17]

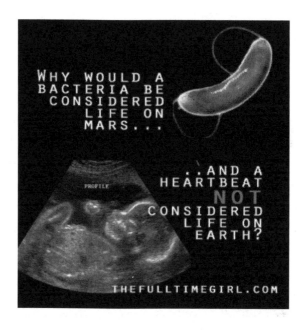

From the brilliant blog "Life on Earth" by Lauren DeMoss, of fulltimegirl.com[18]:

> In 2009, NASA scientists had produced the most compelling evidence yet that bacterial life exists on Mars.

"This is very strong evidence of life on Mars," said David Mackay, a senior scientist at the NASA Johnson Space Center.

Just imagine how people would react if they discovered an actual heartbeat on Mars ... and yet, some refuse to admit that a human heartbeat concludes that life begins at conception ... Faye Wattleton, the longest reigning president of Planned Parenthood, argued as far back as 1997 that, everyone already *knows* that abortion kills. She proclaims the following in an interview with *Ms. Magazine*: *"I think we have deluded ourselves into believing that people don't know that abortion is killing. So any pretense that abortion is not killing is a signal of our ambivalence, a signal that we cannot say yes, it kills a fetus."*

In 1981, a United States Senate judiciary subcommittee received the following testimony from a collection of medical experts[19]:

"It is incorrect to say that biological data cannot be decisive ... It is scientifically correct to say that an individual human life begins at conception."—Professor Micheline Matthews-Roth, Harvard University Medical School

"I have learned from my earliest medical education that human life begins at the time of conception."—Dr. Alfred M. Bongioanni, Professor of Pediatrics and Obstetrics, University of Pennsylvania

"By all the criteria of modern molecular biology, life is present from the moment of conception."—Professor Hymie Gordon, Mayo Clinic

"Biologically speaking, *every* abortion at *every* point in the pregnancy ends the life of a genetically-distinct human being."—abort73. com.

The fact that abortions are so common in America today does not make them right. The number of babies now aborted annually in America is close to the number of Jews who were murdered annually in the Holocaust during the Second World War. Please take thirty-three minutes to watch the award-winning *180 Movie* that has changed hundreds of minds and saved countless lives.

"For many years, I have felt frustrated and disheartened with the issue of abortion, wondering how I could really make my voice heard. '180' is an amazing solution in getting our voices out there. We can send a message around the world from our own homes. Not only does it deal strongly with the issue of abortion,

it leaves people with the hope of the gospel of
Jesus Christ! Let's link our arms and fight for,
not only the lives of the unborn, but the souls
of the unsaved." —Rachel (Comfort) Zwayne

In a 2003 report, the National Abortion Federation stated,
"Each year, almost half of all pregnancies among American
women are unintended."[20] Another one of their documents
reads, "Women at risk for poor post-abortion adjustment are
those who do not get the support they need, or whose abortion
decisions are actively opposed by people who are important to
them." [21]

Support they need? Really? What kind of "support" might
that be? People who say, "You did the right thing, honey—after
all, think of the 'freedom' you will have without a child to
parent?"

What about all the heart-broken couples waiting to adopt
a baby?[22] Please, if you are pregnant and are considering
abortion—and for whatever reason you do not feel that you
can keep the baby to raise—*please* choose adoption. As Marvin
Penner said, "The baby is the answer to someone's prayers."[23]

CHAPTER 16

My Hope

P ost Traumatic Stress Disorder (PTSD) has become a well-known issue that war veterans sometimes deal with, but not everyone knows that post-abortive women deal with many of the same symptoms, like Janice and I did.

Theresa Karminski Burke, Ph.D., is a psychologist and founding director of Rachel's Vineyard, a national organization focused on post-abortion recovery. In a March 1994, she wrote an article for Rachel's Vineyard Ministries entitled, "Abortion and Post Traumatic Stress Disorder: The Evidence Keeps Piling Up."[24]

In this article, Burke wrote:

> Many misquote former Surgeon General Koop as saying that there were no adverse psychological effects of abortion on women. What Dr. Koop actually said, in a three-page letter to then-President Reagan, was that available studies were flawed, because they did not examine the problem of psychological

consequences over a sufficiently long period. He recommended that millions of dollars be spent on investigating this area. Yet "choice" advocates and the present administration have consistently blocked governmental funding of these research efforts.

Certainly, not all women experience emotional problems following induced abortion. However, since Koop made his statement, an alarming amount of evidence has accumulated that, for some women, abortion is responsible for a broad array of deep psychological and emotional disturbances. Unfortunately, these women keep their pain to themselves. According to one study, three out of four people surveyed keep sexual secrets, like abortion, from their partners—and even sometimes from themselves. By not acknowledging a traumatic abortion experience, a psychological barrier is erected and an emotional toxicity is perpetrated. A woman may experience—coupled with denial and avoidance—numbing, amnesia, phobic responses and interpersonal distancing. For this reason, elective abortion remains one of the most emotionally charged and politically sensitive topics worldwide.

In the aftermath of abortion, however, the woman has no place to process her trauma. She has had a grim, painful, perhaps frightening experience—and she can't talk about it. There is little social support for women who find abortion a stressful experience. There is no validation for her grief and anger. After all, it was her choice. From pro-life group she may feel she hears, "You murdered your baby; how did you expect to feel?" From pro-choice groups, she may be told, "It's your body, and it was your decision. It was just a piece of tissue, and there is no reason to feel bad."

She concludes her article by saying:

> The fierce battlers for abortion rights are blindly dismissing the many women whose lives are being destroyed by the solution they chose to an unplanned pregnancy. Such an attitude displays an uncaring abandonment of reason in favor of ideology. Because the consequences of abortion can be so threatening, we don't want to exacerbate the problem by doubling or negating the many women who have undergone excruciating pain because of the "choice."

The issues of suicidal thoughts, drinking, and bulimia that I dealt with are common among those who have been through an abortion. If you have had an abortion and experienced any of these things, know that you're not weird, you're not alone, and God wants to heal every part of you.

For the remainder of this chapter, I would like to do some soul searching with you. May I ask you some questions? Let me begin by asking: have you felt your heart pounding at any time while reading my story? What specifically has touched you and why?

Have you had an abortion—or two—or more? If so, I pray in the name of Jesus that you find your identity, salvation, forgiveness, and emotional freedom in Christ. It's possible—it has happened for me. My prayer for you is taken from the Bible:

> *That He would grant you, according to the riches of His glory, to be strengthened with might through His Spirit in the inner man, that Christ may dwell in your hearts through faith; that you, being rooted and grounded in love, may be able to comprehend with all the saints what is the width and length and depth and height—to know the love of Christ which passes knowledge; that you may be filled with all the fullness of God. Now to Him who is able to do exceedingly abundantly above all that we ask or think, according to the power that works in us, to Him be glory in the church by Christ Jesus to all generations, forever and ever. Amen.*
> Ephesians 3:16–21 New King James Version

The word *Gospel* means "good news" about Jesus Christ. Know that when you ask God to forgive you, the Bible says that He removes our sins as far as the east is from the west. It also says, *"God was in Christ, reconciling the world to himself, no longer counting people's sins against them"* (2 Corinthians 5:19 New Living Translation). Now that is good news!

Have you been involved with performing an abortion? If so, this book is not written to condemn you. Almighty God is a God of forgiveness. Even if you happen to be an abortionist or have assisted with abortion in any way, God wants you to be free—He is the giver of life.

I'm sure many in the medical community have chosen their career for the purpose of helping people. I propose that abortions are hurting far more than helping. Among the synonyms listed in Microsoft Word for the word "abort" are the words, "terminate, end, halt, stop, quit …." To abort means to halt the life of another human being. *Dear God, what are we doing?*

Another issue is gender selection; I am dumbfounded that there is even such a debate! I believe that deformation is no reason to have an abortion either. There are couples willing to adopt even special-needs babies. On the other hand, a friend of mine in Iowa was told by her doctor that her baby would be born with Downs Syndrome and was presented the option of aborting the baby because of that. She and her husband chose to let their baby live and he was born *perfectly healthy* with normal chromosomes and no deformity or abnormality whatsoever! Her son is now a strong, healthy, God-loving young man living out a fully typical life today.

In 2002, our nation was in an uproar when Scott Peterson murdered his pregnant wife. The California court ruled that he committed *double* murder. Now let me ask you, why is it legal for women in California to murder their own unborn babies while men go to prison for doing it? Some may answer that it's because it's *her* body. But that body living inside of her is not her body. The baby has a body of its own with its own blood type, organs, and even the baby's brain begins to form in only the third week of pregnancy.[25] What about the baby's right to his or her body? Under the "it's my body and I can do what I want with it" debate, isn't it wrong for a mother to not allow her baby the right to make his or her own decisions about his or her own body? As I saw for myself in the clinic when I had my abortion, the baby's body is not the mother's body. The baby has its own body.

Can you see how ridiculous this is? Our states set rules all the time on what we cannot do with our bodies. Case in point: seatbelt laws mandate what we do with our bodies. We must buckle up. Or, how about having to take an alcohol breathalyzer test? Limits are set as to how much alcohol a person can consume and still get behind the steering wheel. These limits and drug laws have been established to protect people from harming themselves and others. Seriously, when will mothers and legislators wake up and admit that unborn children, from the point of conception, are indeed in that class of "others" and deserve to be legally protected? They should be protected from the point of conception—not just beginning midway through a pregnancy, or during the last trimester, or during birth—or any other phase thereafter than from the very start.

Regarding the issue of saving a mother's life during childbirth, with our medical knowledge these days, even babies born extremely prematurely still have a fighting chance at life.

There are far too many thousands of people in our world aching to adopt a baby. If you are pregnant and cannot raise the child yourself, please give the baby up for adoption. *Please.*

Have you been raped? This question is not only for women. *Men have been raped too.* In fact, "Two point seventy-eight million men in the U.S. have been victims of sexual assault or rape," according to the National Institute of Justice and Centers for Disease Control and Prevention.[26]

God is offering you freedom from your past so that the past can *be the past at last.* He wants you to be able to walk free in your present and to be confident in your future. I urge you to get help. There are reputable resources listed in the back of this book of people who are far better equipped than my high school "counselor" was.

Have you raped someone? God is a God of mercies that are new every morning and His faithfulness toward you is great. Don't you want to get help immediately and STOP the cycle before it happens again? Before your hands even let go of this book, pick up the phone and call for help. Make today the day to take responsibility and get assistance.

Have you been suicidal for any reason? If so, put down the weapon! Replace suicidal thoughts by putting God's Word into your eyes and ears. The following verses from the Bible are a good place to begin:

> *For You* [God] *formed my inward parts; You covered me in my mother's womb. I will praise You, for I am fearfully and wonderfully made; marvelous are Your works, and that my soul knows very well. My frame was not hidden from You, when I was made in secret, and skillfully wrought in the lowest parts of the earth. Your eyes saw my substance, being yet unformed.*
> Psalm 139:13–16 New King James Version

> *If your heart is broken, you'll find GOD right there; if you're kicked in the gut, he'll help you catch your breath.*
> Psalm 34:18 The Message

> *The LORD is close to the brokenhearted; he*
> *rescues those whose spirits are crushed.*
> Psalm 34:18 New Living Translation

> *He heals the brokenhearted and binds up their*
> *wounds.*
> Psalm 147:3 New King James Version

> *Give all your cares to the Lord and He will give*
> *you strength.*
> Psalm 55:22 New Life Version

> *For I know the thoughts that I think toward you,*
> *says the LORD, thoughts of peace and not of evil,*
> *to give you a future and a hope.*
> Jeremiah 29:11 New King James Version

> *Surely, there is a future, and your hope will not*
> *be cut off.*
> Proverbs 23:18 New American Standard Bible

I can't stress enough the importance of getting help. You don't have to fight this battle alone. The telephone number for the National Suicide Hotline (and Veteran's Crisis Line) is 1-800-273-TALK (8255). Or you can visit their Web site: suicidepreventionlifeline.org.

Suicide is never the right answer. No matter how big of a mess we make of our lives, God Almighty is in the cleanup business, and He is good at it. You can trust Him to help you with whatever mess may seem "immovable" under the rugs of your life. He delights in making your mountains become smooth highways, causing beauty to come from ashes, and turning your mourning into dancing. (See Isaiah 45:2, 61:3, and Psalm 30:11.)

Do you know for sure that you will go to heaven when you die? If you are not sure where you will spend eternity, you can make the choice right now to invite Jesus Christ to be your Savior and Lord. Salvation is not a "hope so" issue. You can *know*. The Bible says, *"These things I have written to you who believe in the name of the Son of God, that you may* know *that you have eternal life"* (1 John 5:13 New King James Version, emphasis added).

There isn't a person alive who hasn't sinned. (See Romans 3:23.) We all need to be saved. Jesus said in John 14:6, *"I am the way, the truth, and the life. No one comes to the Father except through Me"* (New King James Version). Jesus is the One who said that He is not *a* way, *a* truth, or *a* life. He said He is *the* One. *The* truth. *The* life. And He loves *you!*

Receiving salvation is not difficult. Romans 10:9–10 tell us, *"If you confess with your mouth that Jesus is Lord and believe in your heart that God raised him from the dead, you will be saved. For it is by believing in your heart that you are made right with God, and it is by confessing with your mouth that you are saved."* (New Living Translation).

Even if you do not connect with anything else I have said, know that God has a plan for your life—and it is good! If you are one of the fortunate few to have made it this far without any residue sticking to your shoes, perhaps you can be used by God to bring hope to others. Purpose today that you will be that person to light up someone else's life. There has been far too much death and pain.

Have you lost a child due to death, miscarriage, stillbirth, or any other means? I am so *profoundly* sorry to all my friends and family members who have not been able to conceive naturally or who have lost children. I ache for what I have done, especially when I have seen the heartache that you have experienced. I grieve deeply with you and continue to keep you in my prayers that you experience God's goodness. A great blog to read on the subject is 10kreasons.wordpress.com by Sarah Blount. Sarah and her husband experienced a stillbirth, and her blog is a beautifully written journey of the recovery process that God is leading them through.

Are you a church leader? Please, with everything that is within me, I ask you to prayerfully consider how you respond to those in any kind of sin—especially those closest to you. God's grace is amazing enough for *anyone* to be set free of any sin—including you.

There is a wonderful Bible story in John 8:1–11 (New Living Translation) in which Jesus sets the example for us to follow when we discover another's sin:

> *Jesus returned to the Mount of Olives, but early the next morning he was back again at the Temple. A crowd soon gathered, and he sat down and taught them. As he was speaking, the teachers of religious law and the Pharisees brought a woman who had been caught in the act of adultery. They put her in front of the crowd.*
>
> *"Teacher," they said to Jesus, "this woman was caught in the act of adultery. The law of Moses says to stone her. What do you say?"*

They were trying to trap him into saying something they could use against him, but Jesus stooped down and wrote in the dust with his finger. They kept demanding an answer, so he stood up again and said, "All right, but let the one who has never sinned throw the first stone!" Then he stooped down again and wrote in the dust.

When the accusers heard this, they slipped away one by one, beginning with the oldest, until only Jesus was left in the middle of the crowd with the woman. Then Jesus stood up again and said to the woman, "Where are your accusers? Didn't even one of them condemn you?"

"No, Lord," she said.

And Jesus said, "Neither do I. Go and sin no more."

Jesus isn't condemning anyone—I don't want to either. I do see that Jesus added, "Go and sin no more," but it starts with forgiveness and accepting His wonderful and amazing grace. Christians should be in the restoration business.

Are you or someone you know too drunk? The Mayo Clinic urges: If someone you know passes out from drinking alcohol, call 911. If the person is conscious, call 800-222-1222 (in the United States) and you will automatically be routed to your local poison control center. The staff at the poison control center or emergency call center can instruct you as to whether you should take the person directly to a hospital. All calls to poison control centers are confidential.

Do not leave an unconscious person alone. While waiting for help, do not try to make the person vomit. Alcohol poisoning affects the way a person's gag reflex works. That means someone with alcohol poisoning may choke on his or her own vomit or accidentally inhale (aspirate) vomit into the lungs, which could cause a fatal lung injury.

Whatever your situation is, it's not the end! God still has a plan for your life and as my mother-in-law says, "God will make your past be the past at last."

I can now sing the old hymn with a consciousness of God's true "Amazing Grace," and I pray that you, too, can know our mighty God's tender loving kindness and mercy toward you. It is available to you the moment that you ask Him.

CHAPTER 17

Does It?

"Everything happens for a reason" is the phrase I most detest. When I hear people say that, it seems to me that what they mean is that for some cosmic purpose, Sovereign God is the *cause* of *everything* that happens in the world. Nothing could be further from the truth. From cover to cover—Genesis to maps—every Bible story has to do with people making choices of their own. Obedience is a common thread; God does not force His will upon us.

In the opening act of the Bible, we see God warning Adam and Eve not to eat of the fruit of the tree of the knowledge of good and evil or they would die. Interestingly enough, it was the only thing God told them *not* to do. Unfortunately they chose to disobey. They did not immediately die physically, but spiritual death—or separation from God—took place and physical death did follow. God didn't *make* Adam and Eve disobey; God did not puppeteer their food consumption, He gave them the choice to make that decision. *They chose* to do their own thing. If their sin happened for a reason designed by God, then God would have been unjust when He called it sin, right?

At one point in the Old Testament, the nation of Israel pleaded with God to have a king like every other nation. They persisted even after God reminded them that He, as their God, was all they needed. He proceeded to warn them about what would happen if they chose a man to rule them, but He let them choose. How did that work out for them? Not so well. It was not God's will that they have a king; it was the will of the masses.

God still let them make their own choice.

The word *if*—which indicates choice—is in the King James Bible over 1,400 times, and the Bible mentions too much about man's obedience to mean that God *causes* everything that happens in everyone's lives.

Without question, I've paid dearly for my choice to abort. God has not punished me—Jesus took that punishment for me on the cross. Nevertheless, I have suffered greatly because there have been a multitude of negative consequences that have taken place as a result of *my* decision.

Neither God nor the devil can control anyone without their permission. That's why we pray—we invite God into our situations. If everything happened for a reason that God was causing, then we wouldn't have to pray about anything. I agree with the catchphrase "everything happens for a reason" in the sense that events do happen in our lives for a reason—but not necessarily a purpose.

Let me explain: The reason is not always because *God* caused the thing to happen. Here are a few reasons I believe events do take place: (1) God steps in and rescues us. (2) God engineers our steps, as in the case of Scott finding me in Tulsa. Even then Scott still had to choose to obey God and move back to Tulsa. Scott also had to listen to God's guidance regarding where to go to church, et cetera. Scott still had to make the choice to ask me out. God had a plan, but *Scott* had to follow God's leading, and so did I. (3) God's enemy Satan shows up on the scene in the form of negative circumstances that affect us adversely. (4) We make our own choices, each with its own set of natural consequences, be they positive or negative. Everything *does* happen for a reason, I happen to believe that it's just not true that *God* causes everything in our lives to happen.

American schools are now filled with anti-bullying seminars. Bullying is a genuine issue in our nation that we aggressively seek to stop. If God is a bully who pushes Himself into our business and bullying is wrong, why would we turn around and celebrate Him? Before anyone says of my story, "Everything happens for a reason—look how it turned out well in the end; people's lives are being touched," I must reiterate that *I* made the choice to have an abortion. Now God, in His infinite goodness, has turned the situation around for good, but He in no way, form, or fashion controlled me to make that choice. Abortion is *not* His will! The choice to kill is against everything He stands for—it's one of His Ten Commandments, "Thou shall not kill." (See Mark 10:19.) His heart breaks over every life lost. Jesus calls death an enemy. (See Matthew 18:34 and 1 Corinthians 15:26.)

The Bible does say that there is one who does steal, *kill,* and destroy, but Jesus called him "the thief." Jesus, in sharp contrast, said that *He* came so we could have *life*—and have it more abundantly. (See John 10:10.) Let there be no confusion. God is good; the devil is evil. Each has a plan for our lives. It's up to us to choose which plan to follow. Choose God's plan and your life will be filled with blessing. Choose the enemy's plan, and you will reap negative, painful consequences.

Here's another phrase that some say: "God won't put anything on you that you can't handle." With that thinking, it is as if God is the One who put the abortion—and rape—experience on me. Perhaps that philosophy comes from 1 Corinthians 10:13, which says, "God is faithful, *who will not allow you to be tempted beyond what you are able*, but with the temptation will also make the way of escape, that you may be able to bear it" (New King James Version, emphasis added). This verse has been completely distorted. First of all, the subject of this verse is *temptation*. Who is the tempter? It certainly isn't God. We know this because James 1:13 states, "Let no one say when he is tempted, 'I am tempted by God'; for God cannot be tempted by evil, *nor does He Himself tempt anyone*" (New King James Version, emphasis added).

Can you see how certain Bible verses have been twisted into erroneous thinking? Before we buy into certain accepted concepts and phrases, let's examine their source and their context to make sure our thinking is correct. If we don't, we can end up believing something completely the opposite of what is true.

God did not choose the abortion for me; I did. God did not choose the rape, my "friend" did; and I was the one who chose to pick up the Solo cup filled with alcohol and drink it. But thank God for His goodness and mercy! He is willing to turn any messes we make into good when we pray and trust Him. I believe that out of my dark story God will bring good to the lives of others; but not because it was *all* a part of His plan.

Our government *and* God allow us the choice as to what to do with our bodies. But here's a fact that is simply beyond my scope of comprehension. Did you know that the courts recognize that *life* undeniably exists within *sea turtle eggs* and have crafted laws to protect that life? How ironic it is, then, that those same courts have also waved a wand for the entire nation to readily dispel of life inside the womb of a human woman. Where is the justice in that?

You and I were given our own lives by God to do with as we please. But that privilege comes with great responsibility. I want to do something significant with the life I have been granted by my parents and my God. I have chosen to use this life to tell others about our *good* God—of His salvation, forgiveness, healing, and unfailing love. He is the giver of *life!*

Now that you have read my story, I hope it has given you a fresh perspective and some thoughts to ponder regarding choices. The bottom line of it all is this: please—if you are pregnant—choose life. If you are not in a surprise pregnancy situation, but you know someone who is and is wondering what to do, will you please share my story with them and encourage that woman or girl to choose life? I believe that you—and the yet unborn child—will be glad you did.

No Matter How Small[27]
by Debbie Seaborn

People are people, no matter how small.
"Life" isn't measured by how big or how tall.

What? "They're not 'people'? They're too small
to exist?"
Just wait a few weeks: Tiny feet! Tiny fists!

They call you an "it," but we know that's not
true.

137

God gave you life. You're a person—a "Who"!

The unborn are people, being formed, being fashioned.
They're God's handiwork, being delicately crafted.

Yes, people are people, no matter how small.
When you meet little "Who," it'll be worth it all!

Afterword

When I chose to have an abortion, I never imagined the long-lasting impact it would have on my mind. For years every baby that was strolled past me at the mall prompted the thought that I should put my story into print. I was just not certain that I wanted the people who actually knew me to know the truth ... about the "real Kristan." This was especially true regarding my Jesus-loving grandmother—I thought what I had done would "kill her."

I first thought about exposing this part of my life when I attended Rhema (pronounced RAY'-muh) Bible Training College in the 1980s—where shattered fragments of my heart began to be melded back into place. But I wasn't courageous enough back then; I was still working through too many issues. I've been called "brave" by so many people for publishing this book, but the real courageous ones are those who have opted to let their untimely pregnancies progress to full term and have chosen to bring forth the lives growing within them. Through the heroic decisions of these women, they have given the gift of life to the innocent babies inside them. The lifestyle and social and financial challenges that accompany that choice are something I will never know firsthand. You are the people I most admire on earth.

I graduated from Bible school in 1988 and married two years later. The idea of writing such a book stayed with me, but several years into our marriage we started having children, (three children within four years) so I was a little busy.

For now though, I sit allowing you, the daring reader, to do exploratory surgery on my soul and to cast your own judgments.

I am so deeply and overwhelmingly sorry with everything that is a part of my being to all of my friends and the families I know who have tried desperately to conceive a child but are still without one in their homes. So many people in the world experience vast despair in wanting to beget children of their own, and here I am writing a book about abortion.

In front of God, I stand clean and forgiven. But when I stand face-to-face with you who've experienced heartache in the childbearing arena, I am saddened deeper still. Please know I've seen your misery and shared your tears. While your yearning cry is deeply embedded in my heart, I also desire for my transparency to make a difference to some fair maiden who should be living "out loud" as a princess yet finds herself locked in a dungeon of despair.

The reasons for abortion vary, but I dare say that a large number of abortions take place because of the very same reason that I had mine—so no one would know what was done at an inconvenient time. I now want everyone to know my story because I passionately believe there is someone out there who needs to read it and will be touched by what it contains.

Actual names and details in my story have been changed in order to protect the individual's privacy. At the requests of some of the people mentioned, I have used actual names.

What I am learning during my writing process is that people are coming out of hiding and sharing their own stories with me and movies like *October Baby* are hitting theaters. Others' stories echo the haunting I have lived with—the accounts of what they have gone through so parallel every emotion and thought I have had. Yet I dare say, not everyone has discovered the forgiveness and freedom I have found in Jesus Christ. Hopefully that can change with this book. If that's you—if you are still hurting or are haunted by your decision to abort—I pray that you will allow God's Spirit to bring healing to your soul. Perhaps this contents of this book contain some balm you can apply to your wounded heart, and you can breathe again.

Hopefully, someday, you too can help bring healing to someone else.

To you who would never find yourselves in the predicament I did, I pray that you may find something within the content of these words that will aid you in helping others in this situation. And maybe—just maybe—someone's life will be bettered for my being an open book.

How to Say No

by Lindsey Griffith

This list is full of ideas that can help either men or women get out of a high pressured situation.

- Believe it or not, you can just say *no*. Don't worry about his or her feelings. If that person cares about you, he or she will respect you and not push it.
- Tell him or her how important it is to you to keep your word to God. You don't want this to be something you regret.
- "I don't want to yet."
- "I'm not ready."
- "I want you to respect me and my decision on this."
- Ask, "Why now? What's the rush?" Translation ... see if he or she really cares for you. Don't be fooled.
- "I made a promise to myself to wait." If the person doesn't respect that, then he or she certainly is not worth your time.
- "I want you to get tested first." That will make the person think twice and you can have that moment to get out.

- As crazy as this may make you sound, ask, "What would happen if a baby were to be created from this right here and right now?"
- "I'm not in the moooooooood!"
- "I'm not comfortable with this."
- "This isn't how I imagined my first time … let's wait."
- "This is a big deal to me. I don't want it to be casual."
- Here's something radical: avoid being in the situation in the first place by not being alone with someone of the opposite sex. If it comes down to it, there are other things you can do besides get physical.
- Say that you have a curfew. You have to go! And if the person keeps pushing the situation, he or she is a jerk and is after only one thing and will say anything to get it.
- "Uummm, no. I don't want to be a parent quite yet."
- For women, say, "I'm not on the pill, sorry. It's not gonna happen."
- Or, "I'm on my period." (It never fails, unless you use it for several weeks in a row!)
- And finally … when it comes to someone who is romantically interested in you, it's simple. Only pay attention to the person's actions; they speak louder than words.

Recommended Resources

- To give a baby up for adoption, you can call Focus on the Family at 1-800-A-FAMILY or visit heartlink.org.
- For any form of counseling-type reading: cloudtownsend.com.
- For rape counseling: Rape, Abuse and Incest National Network (RAINN):
  1-800-656-HOPE or rainn.org; or visit rapecrisis.com.
- My Bible school: rhema.org.
- Many translations of the Bible: biblegateway.com.
- Movie about the holocaust's dehumanization: 180movie.com.

About the Author

Kristan Gray's utmost favorite job is being the mother of her two sons and her daughter. The money is a little better, however, working as a columnist and staff writer at *The Valley News* in Shenandoah, Iowa. You can read her column, "One More Thing," in the opinion section at valleynewstoday.com. She's also known around the southwest Iowa region as "Kristan Gray from KMA" where she was a morning drive radio news anchor.

From 1988 to 1993, Kristan served as an actress in the show *Fire by Nite*, a Christian program that followed a *Saturday Night Live*-style variety format. It was produced by Willie George Ministries and aired on the Trinity Broadcast Network. The broadcasts were also available through a monthly video club for church youth groups around the world.

Kristan worked in the insurance industry for about a minute but quickly realized stringing words together for a living comes more naturally—and is a much deeper barrel of monkeys—than trying to disseminate government regulations.

One favorite phase of her life was five years spent as a missionary to Africa with her husband, Scott, and her children … but that's a whole different book.

Notes

[1] Karen and Richard Carpenter, vocal performance of "Close to You," written by Hal David and Burt F. Bacharach, released August, 1970, on *Close to You*.

[2] "How to turn down a perfectly good sour sucker," written by Kristan Gray for The Valley News Today in Shenandoah, Iowa on April 27, 2013. Reprinted with permission. See www.valleynewstoday.com/opinion/one_more_thing/how-to-turn-down-a-perfectly-good-sour-sucker/article_75a99f12-0562-567f-bf46-48e5485e244e.html, accessed September 4, 2013.

[3] [3] Donny and Marie Osmond, vocal performance of "Make the World Go Away," written by Hank Cochran in 1963, released 1975.

[4] [4]Donny and Marie Osmond, vocal performance of "Morning Side of the Mountain," recorded 1975, by Manning, Dick/Stock, Larry Lawrence, Lyrics © Warner/Chappell Music, Inc., Memory Lane Music Group, recorded 1975.

[5] Donny and Marie Osmond, vocal performance of "Make the World Go Away," written by Hank Cochran in 1963, released 1975.

[6] Tamar Lewin, "Just 1% of All Abortions," published: October 13, 1989,

www.nytimes.com/1989/10/13/us/rape-and-incest-just-1-of-all-abortions.html, accessed August 21, 2013.

[7] Phillip Keller, *A Shepherd Looks at Psalm 23* (Grand Rapids: Zondervan Publishing House).

[8] William Cowper, "There Is a Fountain," public domain, 1772.

[9] www.nrlc.org/Factsheets/FS03_AbortionInTheUS.pdf, accessed September 4, 2013.

[10] www.cdc.gov/mmwr/preview/mmwrhtml/00031585.htm, accessed August 21, 2013.

[11] Henshaw SK, Unintended pregnancy in the United States, *Family Planning Perspectives*, 1998, 30(1):24–29 & 46.Quoted at www.guttmacher.org/pubs/fb_induced_abortion.html, accessed August 21, 2013.Jones RK and Kavanaugh ML, Changes in abortion rates between 2000 and 2008 and lifetime incidence of abortion, *Obstetrics & Gynecology*, 2011, 117(6):pp-pp. Quoted at www.guttmacher.org/pubs/fb_induced_abortion.html, accessed August 21, 2013.

[12] Jones RK and Kavanaugh ML, Changes in abortion rates between 2000 and 2008 and lifetime incidence of abortion, *Obstetrics & Gynecology*, 2011, 117(6):pp-pp. Quoted at www.guttmacher.org/pubs/fb_induced_abortion.html, accessed August 21, 2013.

[13] See www.youtube.com/watch?v=rY-bQ6UzhNI, accessed August 21, 2013. Uploaded on April 28, 2011.

[14] See thetruth-blog.blogspot.com/2011/05/why-wait-for-marriage.html, Sunday, May 1, 2011, accessed August 21,

[15] See www.180movie.com/, accessed August 21, 2013.2013.

[16] See www.prochoice.org/about_abortion/facts/women_who.html, accessed August 21, 2013.

[17] See gregkoukle.blogspot.com/2010/01/abortion-unborn-human-persons.html, accessed August 21, 2013.

[18] See www.thefulltimegirl.com/2012/10/15/life-on-earth/, accessed August 21, 2013.

[19] Subcommittee on Separation of Powers to Senate Judiciary Committee S-158, Report, 97th Congress, 1st Session, 1981. Quoted at www.humanlife.org/abortion_scientists_attest.php and www.abort73.com/abortion/medical_testimony/.

[20] Guttmacher Institute. Facts in Brief—Induced Abortion. 2003. www.agi-usa.org/pubs/fb_induced_abortion.html.

[21] See www.agi-usa.org/pubs/sfaa.html.

[22] See www.pregnantpause.org/adopt/wanted.htm, accessed August 21, 2013. There are no national statistics on how many people are waiting to adopt, but experts estimate it is somewhere between one and two million couples according to National Committee for Adoption, *Adoption Factbook*. Washington DC: 1989. As quoted in Hsu, Grace. "Encouraging Adoption". Family Research Council: 1995.

[23] www.willistonherald.com/opinion/letters_to_editor/don-t-advocate-abortions-for-others/article_4f17cad2-9c71-11e2-85b3-001a4bcf887a.html, accessed August 21, 2013.

[24] See rachelsvineyard.org/PDF/Articles/Abortion%20and%20Post%20 Traumatic%20Stress%20Disorder%20-%20Theresa%20.pdf, accessed August 21, 2013.

[25] See www.buzzle.com/articles/brain-development-in-fetus.html, accessed August 21, 2013.

[26] "Prevalence, Incidence and Consequences of Violence against Women Survey," 1998. See www.rainn.org/get-information/statistics/sexual-assault-victims, accessed August 21, 2013.

[27] Debbie Seaborn, Used by permission.

Notes

Notes

Notes

Notes

Made in the USA
Middletown, DE
05 August 2015